# YOU GOT THIS

## The ULTIMATE NEGOTIATION GUIDE for PROFESSIONAL WOMEN

### 13 Strategies to Ace Your Next Negotiation

**LELIA GOWLAND**

ILLUSTRATIONS BY

**LAURA SANDERS**

SATTLER
PRESS

To my favorite feminist: T. Cole Newton.
Becoming your life partner didn't take away my
independence; it empowered me to embrace my
strength while feeling completely supported.

It's really fun to be your wife.
Thanks for doing life with me.

To my maternal grandmother, Elise Stille Plauché,
who was smart, loving and feisty as hell.
This book is dedicated to all the women before us
who wanted to do more than their time allowed.
Let's make them proud.

# Table of Contents

# Hey There!

## "Is 100 the right number?"

That's what engineers at NASA asked Sally Ride in 1983, wondering how many tampons she would need for *one week* in space. She told them no, "That would not be the right number."[1]

While you might not face precisely the same challenges as the first American woman in space (and your male colleagues probably aren't asking about your tampon consumption), odds are good that not too long ago in your career, you had a similar, "What?! Did that seriously just happen?" moment.

While women have made tremendous strides since the 1980s, our experience at work and the advice we receive as professionals can often feel ass-backward.

That is certainly true when it comes to negotiation.

Hi! My name is Lelia. I work with women who want to increase their impact and have more fulfilling and profitable careers.

Ever since I attended a "diversity workshop" in high school that focused on women's portrayal in the media, I've geeked out on this stuff. Now with academic chops (a Master's in Public Policy and a BA in Sociology) to back me up, I apply my understanding of political, professional, and cultural systems to support women in the workplace.

In addition to my work as a coach, I write for publications including *Forbes, NBC News*, and *Harper's Bazaar*. As a former teen magazine enthusiast, I was particularly delighted when *Cosmopolitan* and *Marie Claire* profiled me for my strengths-based approach to negotiation.

If you're still looking for reasons to trust me, Fortune 500 companies such as GE and Expedia.com, along with professional associations in fields from auto care to healthcare, have brought me in to support their teams.

My entire business model was precipitated by one phone call.

Several years ago, my dear friend Dina called me for advice. She'd just been offered a role at her dream organization, but the role was a lateral move and provided only a slight salary increase from her then-current gig. She felt conflicted.

During our conversations, Dina worked through the emotions that were coming up for her during negotiations and developed clarity about her career goals. Once she knew what she wanted, we strategized about how to frame the conversation with her prospective employer.

Over the course of the day, Dina had multiple conversations with the hiring manager and with me. By close of business, she had successfully negotiated an improved vacation package, a salary at the top of the company's pay band, and a path to promotion over a specific timetable. With that contract in hand, she enthusiastically accepted the job at an organization that was already aligned with her interests and passions.

When I got off the phone with Dina, I told my then-fiancé, now hubs, "That was so much fun! I wish I could do this for a living. [Shrug.] Oh well, I guess I'll go back to work."

Over the next several months, women continued to come to me informally for support in workplace negotiations and career decision-making.

As I started digging into the available negotiation resources to better support my friends, I realized the available material fit largely into one of three camps:

## Camp 1: Everyone Should Negotiate Like Business Bros Negotiating with Other Bros

At best, this advice encourages decisive communication and an assertive approach, which are techniques that can be helpful for women, too.

At worst, however, this advice is hyper-masculine, even while it implies that negotiations are gender-neutral, which they're usually not. In fact, women often face negative consequences for exhibiting the same behaviors as men. As a result of this double standard, while it might work well enough for men, this "expert" advice for successful negotiation can massively backfire for women.

Not exactly helpful, right?

## Camp 2: Women Should *Always* Negotiate, and Only in *This Specific Way*

There's no shortage of advice for women who work, but too often this advice makes us feel like we're doing it all wrong. The bias we face is our fault, and it's on us to end the wage gap. (In a bit, we'll dig into how deeply flawed and problematic that logic is.)

The other key element of Camp 2 is the wholly unrealistic advice we get about our feelings—that we should experience no emotions in the process of negotiation or ignore the ones we do experience.

Essentially, we're told: You may be discriminated against based on your gender, but as a society, if we're ever going to overcome the wage gap, you *always* have to negotiate. Also, you can't have any feelings about it.

Yikes.

## Camp 3: Women Make Great Negotiators

After digging into the existing research and having conversations with friends and colleagues, I realized women crave a third camp: a space where we can reflect on our priorities, deal with emotions as they come up, and become confident negotiators by developing our own authentic voices.

Within a few months of Dina's call, I changed my business model completely. No longer a full-time Jacklyn of all trades

(AKA, a consultant), I now use my academic and professional experience to support women as they navigate their careers on their terms.

Since each woman's experience in the workplace and the world is affected by multiple, overlapping identities, I'll share some of mine.

I'm a New Orleans native and enthusiast who travels the country speaking about women in the workplace. In practice, this means I spend a lot of time talking with strangers in airports, naturally use the word *y'all*, and have an entire closet dedicated to costuming. It also means that I strive to bring the affirming warmth and *joie de vivre* of my hometown to all of my work.

As I write this, I'm pregnant with a tiny human who my partner and I lovingly call "Little Monster" while he/she/they is in utero.

## A NOTE ABOUT LANGUAGE

When I use the words *women* and *female*, I'm describing folks who identify as female, whatever that means to them. Gender is nuanced and personal. Each person has their own experience, and there's no universal truth about how women (or members of any group) behave. Still, from research and experience, we can observe well-documented trends.

For generations, most of the "women's movement" has focused on women who present the way I do—white, cisgender, heterosexual, well-educated, financially secure. But most people don't fit that mold.

My friend Linette Lopez is a powerhouse finance journalist at *Business Insider* with a wry sense of humor. She's a woman in her thirties who identifies as Afro-Latina. She says, "Every time I meet with a new source, I have to pay a 15-minute tax in which I explain to them why they're sitting across the table from me and not a 50-something-year-old white dude named Barry."

While I have to overcome bias against women and young(ish) professionals, I don't personally know what it's like to navigate racism or the bias Linette might face due to the confluence of her other identities.

My expertise and personal experience focus on gender but consider the other identities that inform your experience: race, socio-economic status, family dynamics, sexual orientation, and more. Each of our identities can impact our expectations about negotiation and the experience we have when we advocate for ourselves. Understanding those impacts can give us the awareness to become thoughtful, strategic negotiators.*

I begin every presentation by showing the audience a picture of my grandmother—first, because my grandmother is a total badass, and second, because she always says, "I'm happy to give you my advice, as long as you promise not to take it." You are the expert in your own life, and you know your context. I'll provide negotiation tools and strategies based on research and experience. Your job is to explore and try to identify what's most authentic and relevant for you.

---

* For insights into the intersections of race, identity, authenticity, and negotiation, check out research from Ashleigh Shelby Rosette, Tina Opsie, and Ruchika Tulshyan—three women of color doing research and consulting with organizations about diversity, equity, and inclusion.

## How to Read This Book

When I was a kid, my orthodontist told me that every night, I had to wear excruciatingly painful rubber bands that wired my jaw shut to correct my overbite. After a few months, he informed me that I had *overcorrected* my bite.

"How often did you wear your rubber bands?" he asked. Confused and annoyed, I told him, "Every night." He maintained that he hadn't actually expected me to wear them nightly.

In case you're like uber-compliant preteen Lelia, let me save you some trouble.

You might be looking at this negotiation guidebook and asking, "Am I supposed to memorize four sections of content and 13 strategies in order to be a successful negotiator? That's a bit overwhelming."

Nope! There's no one "right way" to negotiate or learn new skills, so use this book however you please. Blaze through it in one sitting on a rainy afternoon and see what sticks or dig into the book part by part, marinating on each reflection question with the commitment of an overzealous 12-year-old.

Or leave it in the bathroom to occupy yourself and house-guests when you're otherwise engaged. The world is your oyster!

### ⧙BONUS!⧘☆

Prepping for a specific negotiation or want to be ready when it's time? I've got you covered! This book comes with a Negotiation Toolkit, which you can access online. It includes the cheat sheets, activities, and sample language I use with clients and in my own negotiations.

Download yours at
**www.negotiationfun.com/bonus**

**TO THE FELLAS** ➔ A special "Hey there" to you, too! While the title of this book indicates that it's designed for professional women, people of any gender can benefit from the content. The following negotiation strategies are great tools regardless of how you identify. Besides, learning about women's experience in the workplace might just make you a better ally to your female colleagues, and we need all hands on deck to ensure a more equitable future. **Read on, friend!**

While it's conversational and playful in tone, this book is grounded in current academic research and professional experience. Throughout, endnotes link to some of my favorite studies and sociological research. Feel free to explore. When you see ☼ you'll know it's an example from my clients' and my own experience. Most of our focus will be on negotiating at work, but you'll likely find yourself using these strategies to negotiate everything from your Verizon bill to what to watch on Netflix.

I've worked with thousands of female professionals to help them increase their influence, become stronger leaders, and develop fulfilling careers so they can create lasting impact in their workplaces and communities. I'm thrilled to share these insights with you.

# NOTES!

# Part One

# CONFIDENCE

———

Why You're a Better Negotiator

Than You Think

ne·go·ti·a·tion
/nə.gōsHē'āsH(ə)n/ (n.)
discussion aimed at
reaching an agreement

**F**emale professionals often tell me, "Oh, I'm terrible at negotiation," or "Negotiations make me want to puke."

Similarly, organizational psychologist Michele Gelfand asked a group of men and a group of women to pick metaphors to describe how they felt about negotiating. One group picked phrases like "winning a ball game," while the other picked "going to the dentist."[2] It's not exactly a mystery which group picked which metaphor.

In real-life situations or academic studies, men are more likely to use language that shows they see negotiation as exciting and fun, while women tend to choose words that suggest feelings ranging from a light ick factor to outright fear.[3]

Men and women approach negotiation in at least two significantly different ways. First, men notice opportunities to negotiate more frequently, and second, they like the process of negotiation more. Alternatively, women tend to see fewer opportunities to negotiate and feel stressed about it when they do.[4] For obvious reasons, this impacts our confidence, the outcomes we're likely to achieve, and our future willingness to negotiate.

Now imagine a study that didn't ask participants about their feelings about "negotiation," but instead asked, "How do you feel about discussion aimed at reaching an agreement?"

Y'all, that's it—the definition of negotiation. Whether it's structured or informal, negotiation is just a discussion aimed at reaching an agreement. Rephrased, it's not that scary!

Taking that reframe back into the research, one study found that when women were told they could "negotiate" for higher

**A FEW EXAMPLES:**

**What movie will you watch with a friend, child, or date?**
Negotiation

**Does "vacation" mean relaxing poolside or adventuring?**
Negotiation

**Should the office buy clicky pens or ones with caps?**
Negotiation

---

compensation, they were less likely than men to do so. But, when participants were told they could "ask" for higher compensation, women were just as likely as men to make the request. Because "asking" is more aligned with how women are expected to behave, we often find it less intimidating.[5]

To hell with that. I don't want to use a different word for negotiation. I want to reclaim the word itself.

Negotiation is for all of us. It's not about "asking" for what we need, it's about advocating for what we deserve. It's not selfish. It's about increasing our impact *and* ensuring we have more profitable and fulfilling careers. It's about making the world more equitable.

One workshop participant told me that she was initially hesitant, but that understanding the definition of negotiation fundamentally changed her thinking. She said, "I love discussion aimed at reaching an agreement. I do it all the time, and I'm great at it."

A shift in mindset can be a miraculous and powerful tool not just in your relationship with negotiation, but also in how you perceive your skills as a professional woman.

Researcher Shira Mor and her colleagues studied the idea of "identity integration" and found that women who see their gender and their professional identities as compatible rather than in conflict are more effective negotiators.[6]

When I first read that study, it had me positively giddy. Basically, if you *believe* that being a woman *and* being a kickass professional are totally compatible, you actually *become* a better negotiator.

Across five experiments, women who had "integrated identities" were more likely to advocate for themselves and achieve better negotiation outcomes—and they didn't see negative consequences or social backlash as a result.

The study's authors suggest that rather than focusing on our potential professional disadvantages as women, we "spend time reflecting on how being a woman is compatible with being an excellent professional." They go on to suggest that we can view our "gender identity as a resource rather than a liability at work."

For example, I pride myself on being an effective communicator, a positive trait often associated with women. In negotiations, this means I'm able to articulate my goals while simultaneously asking lots of questions and being solicitous of my counterpart. Consider the ways your gender identity aligns with your professional identity.

**This book is dedicated, in part, to helping you recognize the ways in which identifying as female can align beautifully with being a successful negotiator.**

If you believe
that being
female and
being a kickass
professional
are totally
compatible,
you actually
become a better
negotiator.

# Recognize Opportunities to Negotiate and Celebrate the Successes

Now let's consider the last time you negotiated. When was it?

According to researchers Linda Babcock and Sara Laschever, most women say it's been months since they negotiated.[7] Some women I've worked with say they've never negotiated, and one grad student told me the last time she negotiated was with her parents—to increase her high school allowance.

For the most part, these women are only considering structured negotiations such as buying a car or discussing compensation. The exception was women with little kids, who told the researchers that they negotiate all the time. "Do you want to take a bath now, or do you want to take a bath in 15 minutes? Either way is fine, but you're taking a bath."

The majority of men, meanwhile, say they've negotiated within the previous week. That's because they consider informal transactions and more ambiguous situations negotiations. These informal negotiations include dividing up roles and responsibilities on a project and deciding which vendor to hire for the office coffee service. As Babcock and Laschever explain it, "the men we talked to saw negotiation as a bigger part of their lives and a more common event."

The contrast between how women and men think about negotiation can best be characterized by two types of negotiation: those that are structured and easily recognizable as negotiations and those that are informal and happen with greater frequency and often lower stakes.

## ☼ A STRUCTURED NEGOTIATION

A while back, I had a structured negotiation with "Cecilia," a magazine editor who wanted to print an article I'd pitched.

Because the magazine was a desirable "big name" publication, it didn't surprise me that Cecilia made no mention of price.

Big publications frequently argue that exposure is part of the "payment" they offer writers, and there are plenty of folks who'll write for free.

Generally, I'm not one of them. I wanted to get paid, so I initiated the negotiation by writing, "Here's my standard fee. How does that align with your budget?"*

Cecilia responded that unfortunately, her budget only allowed her to pay me about 1/10th of my rate. She said she understood if I wanted to take my work elsewhere.

I followed up by asking, "Is there any flexibility in that rate?" She replied that there wasn't, and she reiterated that she understood if I wanted to pitch my article to another publication.

Here, I had a decision to make. My thought process went something like this:

- This is a "big get" and will increase my credibility as both a speaker and a writer.
- Since the article is based on a current event, it's time sensitive.
- The pay is so low, it's almost insulting.

While I was disappointed with the fee and felt undervalued, my choice ended up being fairly straightforward. The benefit of the big name far outweighed the financial considerations. I thanked Cecilia for her candor and accepted the reduced rate, fantasizing about my byline as I hit send.

Once the article was public, I was thrilled by the reception it received. Beyond improving my credibility with a name brand publication, the article prompted rich conversations within my social network as well as with readers I didn't know.

---

*I generally advise against negotiating via email because so much is lost in tone. (When you wrote "Sure!" was that enthusiastic? Sarcastic?) Still, in certain instances, such as working with an editor on a quick turnaround article, there's not a viable alternative.

## ☀ AN INFORMAL NEGOTIATION: APPETIZER SUCCESS

In stark contrast to my virtual negotiation with Cecilia, I recently met up with a friend at a delightful Mexican restaurant. Since we hadn't anticipated load-your-own guacamole, we had to make choices quickly about our guac ingredients while the waiter… waited. We both wanted tomatoes and cilantro. I didn't want my mouth to be on fire, so we got jalapenos on the side. He didn't want onion breath, and they weren't a priority for me, so we skipped them. You get the idea. In the end, the guac was the delicious result of a perfectly executed negotiation.

If I hadn't already been thinking about it at the time, I would never have flagged my guacamole experience as a negotiation. But that's exactly what it was. My dinner companion and I had two contrasting views of what constitutes good guac, and we talked it out to create a dish that we'd both enjoy. Thinking of a light-hearted conversation about appetizers this way gives me another data point suggesting that I'm not only good at negotiation, but also that I do it frequently and well.

Informal guacamole-type negotiations happen nearly every day. When you become more aware of these opportunities, you can flex your negotiation muscle more frequently without being too worried about the results.

## Redefine Negotiation Success

While I didn't enjoy my experience with Cecilia the magazine editor when it happened, it did serve as AFOG (Another F***ing Opportunity for Growth).[8] Here's what I learned:

First, if I considered my challenging experience with Cecilia my most recent negotiation, the next time I negotiated would be stressful. I'd see the experience as evidence that I'm a terrible negotiator. Sure, I got the article published, but only by earning one tenth of what I deserved. Oof!

Alternatively, by paying attention to the other times I've negotiated and enjoyed the process (like bargaining about guac ingredients), I can make each new negotiation less scary. As silly and exceedingly low-stakes as the guac example is, think of it as part of a larger picture.

When I focus on the times I have successfully divided up projects with my team, had challenging conversations with clients, and all the other daily negotiations I have navigated successfully, I discover a more accurate—and positive—view of negotiation in my life.

Second, instead of thinking of my negotiation with Cecilia as a failure, I remind myself that I got what I wanted, an impressive byline and published article. This happened because I knew my priorities (publish this time-sensitive article in a major outlet), and I knew my alternatives (keep shopping the article around in the hopes it gets picked up).

**When we actively look for opportunities to negotiate and recognize what we enjoy about negotiation, we're likely to be more effective. Let's celebrate our successes, and maybe even our AFOGs, along the way.**

## Our New Approach

I stand for a new vision of negotiation—one that centers equity, collaboration, and mutual benefit.

No longer is the archetype a group of old dudes in dark suits, greedily manipulating others into doing what they want.

Instead, negotiators are the women rising in leadership in male-dominated industries and lifting up other marginalized voices in the process. Negotiators are the recent grads and grown women who are charting their own paths. Negotiators are our sisters and friends advocating for their advancement and the allies who join them in creating a more equitable future.

We're reclaiming the word *negotiate* as something we do all the time and are pretty damn good at already. Welcome to the team!

## REFLECTION QUESTIONS

- How does identifying as female align with being an effective negotiator for you? What other identities impact your experience?
- Using the definition "discussion aimed at reaching an agreement," when was the last time you negotiated? How many negotiations can you find this week?
- What would your sign say at our Reclaiming Negotiation Rally?
- Follow-up from earlier: How many tampons would you pack for a week in space?

# NOTES!

# Part Two

# PREPARATION

---

Strategies for Before

You Negotiate

# Strategy 1: Identify Your Goals

### Have you ever left a negotiation only to ask yourself, "What the hell just happened?"

I've noticed a pattern when a negotiation goes wrong in my life. Usually, I didn't figure out what my priorities were in advance, I didn't effectively articulate my goals, or worse yet, I've been so concerned about the other person's needs that I forgot to consider what I wanted.

Writing down your goals in advance has two benefits. First, it helps ensure you've thought about what you want and need in a calm state, which is better than scrambling to figure it out mid-negotiation. Second, it provides something tangible to help you stay grounded in your priorities and articulate them.

You can outline your goals without creating rigid expectations. We'll use two negotiation vocab words here to help clarify the process: *position* and *interests*.

A **position** is your desired outcome, or the best way you can think to resolve the negotiation. Alternatively, an **interest** is your underlying goal or motivation, what's important to you in a broader sense.

Here are three quick examples of positions and interests:

| SITUATION | POSITION (desired outcome) | INTEREST (underlying goal or motivation) |
| --- | --- | --- |
| Performance Review | A promotion | Increase my responsibilities and income |
| Client Meeting | Get hired for this project | Make a difference on this issue and get paid |
| Work Schedule | Fridays off | Switch to a four-day work week |

In the first example, my ideal outcome for my performance review is to get a big fat promotion and enjoy the associated salary bump and increase in responsibilities. That's my position, which is informed by my underlying interest.

In the negotiation, perhaps my employer will tell me there aren't any currently available roles at the next pay band or that she wants me to have an additional six months of experience before considering me for the next role. In either case, if I'm exclusively focused on my position, I'm kind of screwed.

Alternatively, if I've gone deeper to identify what's really motivating me (my interest), I'll know that what I really want is more responsibility and money.

When I talk to my boss, I can therefore ask questions to identify other ways I can achieve my goals. Perhaps I can take on a project with new responsibilities or get an additional certification that will boost my salary.

In the second example, if a client comes to me with a social justice oriented-project, I might get really fired up. My position is to get hired. If this particular project doesn't work out, though, it helps to be clear that my priority isn't this project specifically. That's just my position. My interest, rather, is to get paid to do impactful work on social justice issues. With that in mind, I can make the case for the client to bring me in on a future project.

Finally, let's imagine I'm in a negotiation about my work schedule. I might advocate for Fridays off (my position), but I could also be happy with another day off, since my interest is a four-day work week.

## ☀ IT'S NOT ABOUT THE DONUT

A nurse once shared the following example of positions and interests in her workplace negotiations. An older patient came in with diabetes and deteriorating health. When the doctor told the patient that she had to stop eating her daily jelly donut, the patient refused, becoming visibly upset by the time she came to see the nurse.

The nurse asked thoughtful questions and learned that unsurprisingly, the patient's emotional response wasn't actually about the donut. The patient lived alone and her only consistent social interaction came each morning when her neighbor brought over two jelly donuts and two cups of coffee for them to enjoy together.

While the patient's position was resolute ("I will not stop eating my daily jelly donut!"), her interest was really about maintaining meaningful social connection. Similarly, the doctor's position ("Stop eating jelly donuts!") was really in service of the doctor's interest: improve her patient's health outcome.

After a compassionate conversation with the nurse that affirmed the patient could have what was most important to her—connection—the patient agreed to eat half a jelly donut with her neighbor each day. This change marks a significant improvement for both parties, and it occurred because they took the conversation beyond their positions and focused instead on their interests.

| SITUATION | POSITION | INTEREST |
|---|---|---|
| Medical Professionals | The patient should stop eating jelly donuts. | Improve health of the patient |
| Patient | I will not stop eating jelly donuts. | Maintain social connection |

## ☀ NEGOTIATING A NEW JOB

If you were negotiating a new job, you'd want to consider all the factors that impact your work life. While tangible goals like the amount of vacation time are easy to quantify, don't forget about intangible goals like establishing credibility as an expert in your field.

As you make your list and prioritize the areas that are most valuable to you, think of the different facets of the job offer as levers you and your employer can adjust to make this role optimal for you both. For example, if you had the opportunity to make a significant commission, perhaps you'd be willing to accept a lower salary.

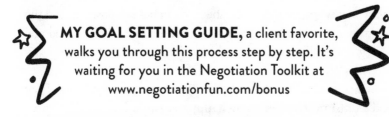

**MY GOAL SETTING GUIDE,** a client favorite, walks you through this process step by step. It's waiting for you in the Negotiation Toolkit at www.negotiationfun.com/bonus

Consider the following questions to help identify your interests: What is my ideal situation? *Why* is that my ideal?

Pretend for a moment that one of your goals is to secure a part-time assistant. If your employer says a part-time assistant isn't possible but instead offers you a corner office and a company car, how you'd reply would depend on your interest.

If your interest in getting an assistant was to impress clients, a corner office and company car could serve as alternative "ooh la la" social markers of prestige. Alternatively, if your interest was to be more efficient at your job, the schmancy car and office would not help you meet your goal.

Focusing on interests helps us avoid getting distracted by what we think we *should* want, or what our counterpart is trying to convince us we want. If you've already defined your goals and interests in writing, you'll be more likely to stay focused in the negotiation. You'll also be better equipped to get creative about alternative ways to meet your interests.

Clarifying what you want *before* going into a conversation is valuable for any negotiator, but it's particularly important for women. Since we're socialized to be concerned about everyone else's well-being, it can be easy to lose sight of our own goals. By starting the negotiation with a clear, written list of goals and interests, you're less likely to be distracted by what doesn't matter to you and more likely to achieve outcomes that do.

## ☼ DON'T "SHOULD" YOURSELF IN THE PROCESS

A client told me she was "in a pickle." She'd gotten a job offer with a salary that was 43% more than she made in her last position, and she felt torn about whether to negotiate for more money. She texted me, "My gut says NEGOTIATE and make Lelia proud, but my head says the salary is awesome and appropriate."

This kind of "pickle" comes up often for my clients. They feel a tension between being happy with an offer and the expectation that they "should" negotiate.

Few words in the English language bother me as much as the word "should."

This particular client was conscious of the wage gap and gender dynamics in the workplace. As we talked through her feelings, she realized she felt a responsibility to negotiate. Even though she had received a fantastic salary offer, the campaigns telling her to "ask for more" made her feel guilt and self-doubt about accepting the role as offered. These well-intentioned campaigns can make us feel like gender bias and the wage gap are our responsibility to fix, when really, they're systemic problems we have to navigate.

Rather than a universal recommendation that women always ask for more, here's what I propose: Do the important self-reflection about your own priorities, and if you choose to, negotiate in a way that feels authentic and comfortable to you.

It's not just employees who have the feels when it comes to workplace negotiations. Former Merrill Lynch CEO and Ellevest cofounder and CEO Sallie Krawcheck describes her own discomfort on the other side of the negotiation table. In her book *Own It*, she writes, "I hate making job offers; even after all these years and all the job offers I've made, I still have an almost physical aversion to doing it, for the fear that the other person will 'get mad' at me that the compensation isn't generous enough. I know...seriously, right?"[9]

You can almost see Krawcheck rolling her eyes in frustration at her own reluctance to make job offers, to negotiate. Yet, she recognizes the discomfort that comes up as part of that process and moves through it. (More on how to do that in *Part 4: Perspective*, which provides strategies for navigating your emotions.)

In practice, there are no easy answers when it comes to navigating workplace dynamics, so try not to "should" yourself about how you feel about negotiation.

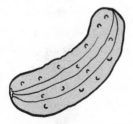

# Strategy 2: Research the Situation and Use Precedent to Your Advantage

Once you have your goals in mind, research comparable situations to help you decide how to frame your goals and figure out what's realistic.

Using precedent gives you a way to show that what you're suggesting is similar to what's been done successfully. It also increases the likelihood that you'll get what you want.

## ☀ SMOKING IN THE BIG EASY

In negotiating the successful passage of the citywide smoking ban in 2015, New Orleans City Councilmember, now Mayor, LaToya Cantrell and her team relied heavily on data from comparable cities that had instituted similar laws. The data assured voters and fellow councilmembers that the ban would have a positive impact on health outcomes and would not adversely affect revenue for restaurants and bars.

When she got pushback, Councilmember Cantrell could point to other cities that had improved respiratory health through the ban and show the world hadn't ended. To be clear, she didn't profess that the Big Easy was identical to Dallas or Ann Arbor. She drew helpful parallels and, when necessary, acknowledged the differences.

### I'm Thinking of a Number...

Often in business settings, "information asymmetry," in which the employer has more information than the employee, puts the employer at an advantage. As a result, when a potential employer asks for your salary range, it can feel like a ridiculously high-stakes guessing game. If you ask for too little, they won't take you seriously, and you'll end up underpaid. If you ask for too much, you'll cut yourself out of the running for the job. Meanwhile, they know exactly what they're looking to pay. No pressure, right?

It doesn't have to be so fraught. You can balance your employer's insider knowledge about how much they want to pay with precedent: your market value in your industry, region, and role. Here are a few strategies for discerning an appropriate range.

### Figure out who's collecting and aggregating the information you seek:

- Many professional associations do audits of salaries in the industry. Even if there's not a formal study, there are still likely people you can chat with about industry trends surrounding salary and benefits.
- Online salary calculators like PayScale (my favorite) and Glassdoor can be invaluable resources in determining your market value and learning more about the company.

Note that searching for salary information based only on a job title and your city won't necessarily give you accurate results. Would you trust a dating app's suggested matches if they were only based on gender and location and there were no pics? You want data that's specific to your education, level of experience, the size of the company you're considering, and more, so be sure you're putting in as much information as possible about yourself and the role to get the most accurate answers. Your final market value report may also include helpful data about benefits.

### Find anecdotal data:

- Networking can be of huge value, but studies show that people tend to network in single sex groups—basically, men network with men, women with women.[10] Remember that thanks to the wage gap, there's a good chance your lady friends are paid less than their male peers. Ugh. Be sure you're talking with both men and women, so you get the most accurate wage information.

- Ask someone who was previously in the role or is familiar with the position, "Would you be comfortable sharing the salary range you think is appropriate for this role based on your experience?" By framing it this way, you're not asking them to disclose what *they* made but are instead asking for their perspective.

Once you're clear on what you want to propose, increase the credibility of your position by demonstrating that your expectations are based on research and precedent. For example, you could say, "Based on my experience and research of positions with a similar level of responsibility and scope in [city/region], I'm seeking a salary range of XYZ."

 **Just having the data isn't enough, though. You also have to *believe* you're worth it.**

By grounding your proposal in research, you set realistic expectations, position yourself well within the negotiation, demonstrate that you're well-informed, and increase the likelihood of reaching a fair offer.

I once worked with a job applicant who through glorious insider intel knew that her prospective employer had budgeted between $90,000 and $100,000 in salary for the role. But when I asked my client about her salary expectations, she told me she was only going to ask for $80,000.

Despite knowing she had been underpaid in her last position and that this role would be a significant increase in responsibility, she felt anchored to her past salary.

We spent significant time together talking through her thinking and working to overcome the self-doubt that told her she didn't deserve her new company's salary range. This situation isn't unique to my client.

Many of us struggle with feelings of self-worth, asking ourselves, "Do I really deserve what I'm asking for?"

The first time I significantly increased my speaker fee, I was nervous. Based on client feedback and a review of other speakers' fees, I knew it was time for the change to match my market value. Still, it was a bit daunting. Prior to making the change, I called a former client who I'd become close to and asked, "You really believe I'm worth this, right?"

Recognize that market value isn't what *you* would pay you. It's the "going rate" for the service or product you provide.

I once heard a story about a woman who sold $16 candles. As she was working with her business coach to increase her rates and profitability, she exclaimed that she would never pay $16 for a candle. She thought it was ridiculous.

Her business coach reminded her that *she* wasn't her target client. In reality, there were plenty of people out there willing to drop 16 bucks for a candle. *Those* were the people who comprised her client base, and they should determine her market value.

With the support of my coach, clients, and colleagues over the last several years, I've nearly quadrupled my speaker fees. With my support, the job applicant who was planning to ask for $80,000 ultimately accepted the new position with a $90,000 salary, a $5,000 signing bonus, and other massive bonuses throughout the year.

If you're feeling uncertain of your worth or uncomfortable with your request, consider talking to a trusted friend, a coach, or a therapist. And remember the candles! Healthy perspective helps.

# Strategy 3: Do a Little Detective Work to Get to Know Your Counterpart

If a friend told you they wanted to set you up on a date with their cousin, what's the first thing you would do? Google the cousin, right? The same should apply to someone with whom you're negotiating. Getting to know your counterpart's interests, what they value, and how they like to receive information can help you decide how to approach the conversation.

Here's an example. Say you want to hire me to write branded content for your organization. Through some light internet creeping, you might learn that another part of my business focuses on public speaking and that my best friend lives in Dallas (I often write about him). If you wanted to request that I decrease my contract fee, you could sweeten the deal by offering me a paid keynote gig at an upcoming conference or by hosting our planning meeting at your Dallas office. Either of these strategies might entice me to accept a lower rate.

You also want to discern what motivates your counterpart at a deeper level. When a friend introduced me to a decision-maker at a major corporation, I looked my new contact up on LinkedIn and learned that she'd spent the past three years on the board of a nonprofit that worked with underserved youth. While her role directing the women's network for her company was the main purpose for our call, we connected on a deeper level when I shared that I had spent a significant part of my career working on juvenile justice issues.

It's about connection, not manipulation. You're striving to meaningfully understand what matters most to your counterpart and demonstrate that you understand. By practicing empathy and building that connection, you can help to create an agreement that focuses on what actually matters to you both.

Once you've gotten a sense of what motivates your counterpart, strive to understand the ways they like to receive information and frame the situation in terms of how it benefits them.

## ☀ SOCIAL JUSTICE VALUES VS. PROFITABILITY

After attending my negotiation workshop, a client who manages a small business wrote to me. She told me that she used the negotiation tools she learned to convince her employer to provide significantly better health insurance subsidies to employees than the minimum required. She wrote, "Using the communication style my employer likes best—reports and statistics—I was able to show why providing extra benefits for our employees based on our demographics would go a long way to prevent turnover."

For my client, this was a social justice issue. Her interest was the well-being of the most vulnerable, lowest paid employees. However, she knew that while her boss cared about his employees, his primary interest was profitability, so she focused on how the change would impact the company's bottom line.

If her boss was instead the type of person who was deeply moved by the personal experiences of his employees, my client would likely have been better off sharing a story about how two hard-working employees became too ill to work because they couldn't access the preventive care they needed.

Getting to know your counterpart and using that information to build sincere empathy can help you understand what motivates them and how they measure success. It will help you focus on their interests rather than their positions, recognize the way they like to receive information, and enable you to frame the negotiation in terms of how it benefits them. All of this will help you go into the negotiation set up for success.

And you thought creeping on your Tinder dates online was a waste of time.

One more story: Eating at Chili's, my friend Mallory told her five-year-old son that he could only order what was on the menu. Wanting bacon for dinner, he drew some on his paper menu and politely asked the waitress for it. The waitress, now his counterpart in the negotiation, said, "Why are you so cute?!" and brought him the bacon. This kiddo knew his audience. The cute factor plus self-advocacy for the win!

## Strategy 4: Know Your Alternatives

In the seminal book on negotiation, *Getting to Yes,* authors Roger Fisher, William L. Ury, and Bruce Patton write, "The reason you negotiate is to produce something better than results you can obtain without negotiating."[11]

You want to go into the negotiation with a clear sense of what you can do if you don't reach an agreement. They call this your Best Alternative to a Negotiated Agreement (BATNA).

For our purposes, we'll call BATNA our "Plan B."

Imagine Plan A is your position: your desired outcome for the negotiation. Your Plan B is your best option if you completely walked away from the table.

There are major benefits to having a Plan B top of mind. For one thing, it's a reminder that you don't have to agree to unfair or unfavorable terms. In fact, you may feel more empowered to negotiate because you know what you'll do if Plan A falls through.

### ☀ CONFERENCE CONNECTIONS

Let's imagine a former client asks me to produce a women's summit. I'm honored and think the gig sounds exciting. That said, planning a summit is a lot of work, and that takes time away from the other aspects of my business.

Before going into the negotiation, I want to reflect on my interests and ensure that I know the qualities I'm looking for in a client. Just because I've enjoyed working with this client in the past doesn't automatically mean producing this women's summit is a good fit with my current priorities.

☆ **Remember, your goals will change with time and new information.**

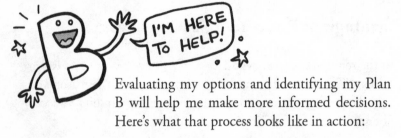

Evaluating my options and identifying my Plan B will help me make more informed decisions. Here's what that process looks like in action:

**1. Explore all the potential actions you could take.**

I'll consider all of the alternative contracts I could pursue instead of this conference. However, while I might *want* to sing backup for Hanson (whom I've loved unconditionally since 1997), for more than a few reasons, it's not a realistic alternative. Instead, I'll consider other ways I could *actually* spend that time instead of producing a summit.

For instance, I could host one of my Career Fulfillment Retreats, try to get hired for a speaking engagement, or devote that time to writing. I could also do nothing. Maybe my finances and schedule will allow for a vacation that week.

**2. Develop the most promising ideas into realistic alternatives.**

For each of the prospects on my list, I'll evaluate how well they meet my interests: impact, income, enjoyment, and opportunities for collaboration.

**3. Evaluate each idea and pick the one that seems best (again, it may be to do nothing).**

Hosting one of my Career Fulfillment Retreats requires a lot of planning, as does producing a summit. With my retreats, however, I know exactly what's required and have a lot systematized. Those retreats are also a great fit with my interests. I've witnessed their impact, and they're typically profitable and super enjoyable. Plus, they offer ample opportunities for collaboration. Planning a Career Fulfillment Retreat is now my Plan B.

Notice that my Plan B is not all of my potential alternatives in the aggregate. Instead, it's one realistic idea that best matches my interests. After all, it's always going to be more appealing to have a bunch of different choices (Hanson road trip, anyone?) than a single realistic option.

### 4. Compare all potential negotiated outcomes to your Plan B.

Once I'm in the negotiation with my Plan B in mind, I'll judge all negotiated agreements or outcomes in terms of how they meet my interests as compared to Plan B. I want to recognize the point at which my Plan B meets my interests better than the current option on the table. Having something specific to compare an agreement to makes it easier for me to recognize a good offer or to know when to walk away.

### CONSIDER YOUR COUNTERPART'S PLAN B.

For this conference, my client's likely alternatives are to:

**Have someone in-house produce the event:** They have a small team and typically hire consultants, so this doesn't seem very desirable.

**Cancel the program:** Since the event has included successful programming for women in the past, cancelling the summit entirely seems unlikely.

**Find another consultant to take on the project:**
This feels most plausible for their Plan B.

Based on these reflections, I'd be pretty confident that I was their first choice. Given my consulting portfolio, intimate knowledge of the organization, and success on previous contracts for them, I'd be optimistic about my bargaining power.

It's helpful to have thought through both my Plan B and theirs before discussions begin.

### It's Ok to Walk Away!

Women are socialized to be relational, so it may feel daunting or not even occur to us to end the conversation without a negotiated agreement. Because you've already put so much energy into the negotiation, you might feel an instinct to continue with it and try to come to a happy conclusion. You can resist this urge by using your Plan B as an anchor to options outside the negotiation.

Deciding whether to walk away can be further complicated when women in male-dominated environments or women who have other marginalized identities negotiate about leadership positions. You may feel added responsibility to be in the room where decisions get made and/or be in a position to lift others up, even if the terms aren't great. There's no perfect solution, so follow your gut and strive to be gentle with yourself.*

If you do decide to end the negotiation, you don't have to leave on bad terms. If you can't reach an agreement but would like to work with the organization or person in the future, you can graciously thank them for their time and ask them to let you know if anything changes.

That said, there may be times when you don't want your counterpart to contact you again. Once, when I was sharing apprehensions about someone I was dating, a friend told me he didn't see any red flags, but a lot of orange ones. Don't ignore those orange flags in negotiation. Consider them data points. Particularly if your Spidey Sense is signaling that your counterpart may be dishonest or treating you with disrespect, entering into an agreement with them may not be the wisest decision, and you may not want to keep any future options open.

Either way, your Plan B can keep things in perspective.

---

*For more on being the only one in the room, my friend and phenomenal writer, Laura Cathcart Robbins, hosts the podcast, "The Only One in the Room." The podcast was inspired by her brilliant, viral article for the Huffington Post, "I Was the Only Black Person at Elizabeth Gilbert and Cheryl Strayed's 'Brave Magic' Retreat."

# Strategy 5: Practice, Practice, Practice

Would you play a piece of music you'd never practiced in front of a packed house at Carnegie Hall? Probably not. The same holds true for a negotiation. You don't want the first time you say the words out loud to be in a meeting with your counterpart. Without preparation, you run a high risk of negotiation word vomit. Role play with a trusted friend, partner, or advisor to help you find language that's comfortable, authentic, and will make your case more convincing.

There are four types of practice negotiations to try with your role play buddy.

## Silly to Serious

Even in a role play, we can get stuck trying to come up with the perfect response. I encourage clients to kick off the practice session with a silly, over the top exchange to get some of that discomfort out of the way. For this exercise, let's assume you've received a first offer from a new employer, and you're negotiating to increase your salary.

You could tell your role play buddy, "This offer is terrible. I expect my new salary to be one million dollars, and I will only work on Tuesdays with left handed people." You and your role play buddy would go back and forth with this silliness for a bit, increasing the ridiculousness to let loose.

When I taught sex ed to middle schoolers, they'd get giggly and wiggly when they were uncomfortable. I'd let them be squeamish for a moment, and then I'd say, "Silly to..." and they'd say, "Serious!" and get settled back into learning mode.

This approach works for adults, too. Follow my fifth-graders' lead: get the silly out of the way so you can get back to business.

# ☆ SILLY ᴛᴏ SERIOUS TRIAL RUN ☆

Fill in the prompts, then flip the book to match your answers
with corresponding numbers on the silly script below.
Read the script aloud with confidence!

1. Who is your favorite athlete?
_____

2. How many pounds do you think the Statue of Liberty weighs?
_____

3. What's one adjective you would use to describe a toddler?
_____

4. How long should someone wait to reach out after a great date?
_____

5. What is your favorite animal?
_____

6. What is your favorite beverage?
_____

7. What famous person would you most like to meet in real life?
_____

8. What is your favorite dessert?
_____

☆ The Script ☆

I am the 1. _____ of my field. I expect a
signing bonus of 2. _____ dollars. I will only join your
team if every 4. _____ I get to 3. _____
sit with a 5. _____ , drink a 6. _____ ,
and see 7. _____ get hit in the face with a
8. _____ .

## Nightmare Scenario

After you've gotten the giggles out, talk with your role play buddy about your biggest fears and worst-case scenario. As scary as it might be, act it out.

Many women I work with worry that their employer will think they're selfish, greedy, or entitled if they advocate for themselves. To work through this within the role play, you could share your salary expectations and have your buddy reply with something awful. They could say, "What makes you think you're worth that? I can't possibly consider that salary or even take you seriously now that you've suggested it." (Ouch.)

Once your counterpart is finished with their nasty reply, keep going! In this low-stakes setting, see what it feels like to think on your feet and respond in real time. You might say, "Hmm, that's surprising given my market research. Would you share more about how you determined the salary range you have in mind?"

Consider what scares you most about negotiation. If you're afraid that you'll forget all of your market research and just spew all of your insecurities, try that route.

Once you've gotten your worst-case scenario out of the way, you'll see how unlikely it actually is—and if by some fluke it happens, you know that you'll survive.

## Realistic Scenario

Once you've tried a silly version and a horrifying one, approach the conversation the same way you'd like to in real life.

You might ask, "Is there any flexibility in the salary offer?" or "Based on my research, I'm seeking a salary of X. Are you open to a conversation about compensation?"

Your initial exchanges might sound something like, "Ummm, what? Errr. Sure...ok. Maybe this salary-ish?" Better to knock that awkwardness out in the role play than in real life.

I recommend trying a few rounds of this to get comfortable with your language and practice adapting to the various directions the conversation could go. Encourage your role play buddy to ask new questions each time so you can listen and reply as you would in real life. They could ask things like, "How did you come up with your salary range?" or "Would you accept [# only slightly higher than the original offer]?" They might even say, "This is the best we can do."

Keep practicing until your responses feel organic and conversational, and don't forget to take breaks as needed.

## In Their Shoes

Finally, hit the reset button. Ask your role play buddy to pretend to be you, so that you can imagine the situation from your counterpart's side. What questions would they have? What would they want to know? What might they be reluctant about?

Playing the role of HR manager, you might say, "Fairness and equity are top priorities for us. We can't pay you more than your colleagues in comparable positions across the company. Our current offer is at the top of our pay band for this role. What if I included a signing bonus or a moving stipend?"

You might realize your counterpart's priorities by engaging in the conversation from their vantage point.

Practicing your negotiation in advance using these tactics can give you new perspective and better language. Just hearing the words come out of your mouth can help you be more confident when it matters.

## ☀ PRACTICE DOESN'T MAKE PERFECT, BUT IT HELPS

When Sasha hired me to consult with her about negotiating a new position several years ago, she told me she had never negotiated a salary and was woefully underpaid in her current position. She was in the midst of the interview process for a new job. Fortunately, they hadn't yet discussed compensation.

Sasha knew that when an employer asks about a prospective employee's salary history, it can perpetuate the wage gap. (In fact, the practice is illegal in several states.) She also recognized that if she disclosed her current salary, she might be at a particularly large disadvantage. In addition to being underpaid in her current role, the job she was applying for entailed a significant increase in responsibility. It was also in an entirely different industry. Basically, the trifecta—and it meant she could end up barely being compensated for taking on a whole bunch of new responsibilities.

She wanted to be paid based on the work she would be doing in the new role, not what she was currently making. However, she was nervous about how to avoid the question if she was asked. So, we practiced.

We talked through sample language like, "My current employer considers that information confidential," and "I only share that information with my accountant." While it felt a little funny for her at first, I'd play the role of HR manager, and Sasha practiced answering the question in her own words until she was more comfortable.

Sasha still wasn't excited about the prospect of the conversation but felt better having a plan. With a better understanding of how this might play out, she decided that the potential for a significant salary increase was worth her discomfort in the interview.

Having looked at salary calculator data and talked with others in the industry to determine the going rate for the position, Sasha knew her market value. (She'd put *Strategy 2: Research the Situation and Use Precedent to Your Advantage* into action.)

In case the HR manager continued to push for her salary history, Sasha practiced acting like a political candidate by pivoting to the question she wished they would ask. She planned to use language that may be familiar: "Based on my research [into the competitive salaries for this position], the range I'm seeking is XYZ. How does that align with what you're thinking?"

Sure enough, in the first interview the HR manager, Amy, asked about Sasha's current salary. Sasha used the language we'd practiced, and they moved on with the interview without her answering the question.

However, it was clear to Sasha that Amy was going to keep inquiring about her salary history, so Sasha asked me, "If Amy brings salary history up again, can I just tell her?" Of course, that was her choice, as I told her, but I still recommended she try to avoid it.

We planned for how Sasha could frame her salary in the event that Amy kept asking until Sasha felt like she had to answer. Sasha planned to reference being underpaid directly and say something like, "I accepted my current salary in part because the company provides extensive other benefits like stipends for my car, cell phone, etc. At this point in my career, I'm only considering positions in the range of XYZ."

Because Sasha recognized her nervousness and practiced (out loud!), she was able to successfully avoid the salary history question completely. Later in the interview process, each time she was asked, she pivoted to the more relevant question: the salary she was seeking.

Using the strategies that we had discussed, Sasha wound up making 30% more than she had in her previous position, in addition to significant bonuses. She and I both believe an increase of this size would have been unlikely had her new employer learned how much she was making in her previous position.

**Sasha's situation worked out splendidly, but a 2017 PayScale survey has shifted the way I talk about sharing salary history.**[12]

PayScale asked 15,000 people who had received job offers whether they were asked to disclose their current pay and whether they shared the information.

When women refused to share their current salary, they made 1.8% *less* than women who answered the question. To add insult to injury, if a man refused to disclose, he got paid 1.2% *more* than men who provided their pay history.

These results were unexpected. As Lydia Frank, VP of Content Strategy for PayScale, says, "When I first saw the numbers I thought, 'Is this right?' Then it started to make a ton more sense for me. If a woman is asked a question and refuses to answer, how does the recruiter feel about that? What assumption do they make—do they assume she is earning a lower salary than someone willing to share their number?"

Frank acknowledges gender bias may be impacting women's experience. There's a social cost to negotiating, namely, neither men nor women like it when women negotiate, she says. "For a woman, it may feel impolite that they don't answer [the salary history question]. With a man, maybe it's seen as confidence. Unconscious bias could certainly be at play here."

This data makes it challenging for women to know how to proceed. "It's so frustrating that I've been telling women not to reveal their salary history, and maybe that's not the right thing," Frank says. "What really needs to be the message here is to push employers to stop asking the question."

Until we have further research, this is what I advise women to do:

## Don't Anchor *Yourself* to Your Current Salary

The main reason I tell women not to share their current pay is because I don't want the employer to anchor or get attached to the number the candidate was previously paid. However, as Frank described it, even if you're not disclosing your current salary, *you* could be anchoring your salary expectations to that lower number.

Do your best to completely separate what you're currently making from what you expect to make in this new role. Your past salary has nothing to do with the work you'll be doing in your new job. Learn your market value using the tools we discussed in *Strategy 2: Research the Situation and Use Precedent to Your Advantage.*

## Make the Decision That's Right for You

You may not end up being asked about your current salary. While it can feel like a pervasive question, only 43% of PayScale's 15,000 respondents were asked about their salary history in their interview processes. It is helpful to know, however, that people interviewing for higher level positions with higher salaries were more likely to be asked.

When it comes to answering, do the important self-reflection about your own priorities and comfort level with sharing your salary history. Know that each situation is different, and you may decide to share with one company but not another. That's ok. Be gentle with yourself and do what feels right for you.

## If You Do Share Your Current Pay, Pivot Quickly to the New Position

I'm a firm believer that you should be paid based on the work you'll be doing in the new role, your new company, and your market value, *not* what you were previously making.

According to Frank, "What you make currently shouldn't matter." Regardless of whether you share that information, she says, "The important thing is to get to the value of the position you're discussing as quickly as possible."

If you decide to share, you can pivot immediately by saying something like, "I'm currently making [$$]. Based on my research into the competitive salaries for this position, the range I'm seeking is [$$$]. How does that align with what you're thinking?" And if you don't want to share your history, you can answer the same way, just cut that first line.

Whether you decide to share your current salary or keep it to yourself, don't dwell on it too much, and try not to feel guilty for whatever decision you make. When it comes to tackling the salary history question, there's no right answer. The important thing is to make a decision and focus on your market value in this new role.

## REFLECTION QUESTIONS

- Often in a negotiation, your *interests* will stay the same, but your *position* may shift as you learn more about what's on the table. How could you see this playing out in an upcoming negotiation?
- How can you use precedent to your advantage?
- What kinds of helpful information might you be able to find about your negotiation counterpart?
- Who could you enlist to be your role play buddy? If you could enlist anyone in the world as your role play buddy, who would you pick? (I'd go with Amy Poehler.)

NOTES!

# PRESENCE

---

Strategies for During

the Negotiation

# Strategy 6: Time Your Negotiation Strategically

When I was growing up, the local skating rink was *the* coolest place to celebrate your 12th birthday. Two-thirds of the way through the party, the staff, who all wore referee uniforms, would initiate a massive game of Red Light/Green Light.

To start, we would skate as fast as our prepubescent legs could carry us until a ref yelled, "Red light!" at which point, we came to a screeching halt. The more talented among us would crouch on our skates' brakes, poised to launch into motion at full speed when the ref declared, "Green light!"

With mediocre balance and a precarious relationship with gravity, I was absolutely terrible at this game and found the entire enterprise stressful, to say the least.

Negotiating at work can feel a lot like this horror-show of a children's game, but without the ref to let you know precisely when the light changes.

**The good news is that the cadence of your negotiation doesn't have to be anxiety producing, and in many instances, you can determine when to initiate the conversation and when to delay it. You're the ref!**

## Green Light: When to Initiate Your Negotiation

Whenever possible, begin negotiations when your counterpart is primed to give you the answer you want. Ideally, you can go into the meeting confident that they have the bandwidth to consider your proposal and are generally feeling favorable toward you.

Just because you decided last night that you deserve a raise doesn't mean that today is the day to ask for it. If a huge report is due next week, or your boss is in a horrible mood after enduring a bunch of expensive dental work, it may not be the best time to advocate for what you want.

In many instances, initiating a salary negotiation means creating more work for your counterpart. Your boss may have to talk with HR or move money to make it work. If your boss is wearing her grumpy pants or seems like she's stretched thin, consider waiting.

In addition to making sure that your boss is in good spirits, you also want her to have the warm fuzzies toward you as you make the request. If you've just landed a big client or given a successful presentation to a funder, now may be a great time to ask for a raise. Ideally, you want to have recently demonstrated that you are an effective, successful member of the team.

Another way to evaluate when to start the negotiation is by asking yourself, "Why now?" Perhaps you've just achieved a professional success, received a positive evaluation, or taken on an expanded workload.

## Red Light: When to Delay the Negotiation

Ever been in the midst of a challenging conversation, and later (perhaps while washing your hair) have an epiphany and think of what you wish you'd said?

When you're in the midst of a negotiation—or a fight with your partner, for that matter—it can be hard to remember that you don't have to keep talking until everything is decided. Stepping back can be helpful. In the moment, you may not have the presence of mind to articulate what you want or to ask important follow-up questions.

Now let's switch gears to negotiating a new position. While we don't often describe it as such, going through the hiring process is essentially one giant negotiation: you want them to hire you, but they're investigating alternatives. Usually, when you get the offer is the perfect time to strategically delay a negotiation.

The moment HR calls with the good news, before you've had a chance to take a breath, it can be tempting to cheer and say, "When can I start?" Resist the urge to immediately say yes. Instead, you could say something like this: "Thank you so much. I'm excited about the potential to work together. Would you send me the offer in writing so I can review the full package? When do you need an answer?"

**RED LIGHT LANGUAGE:**

Are you open to continuing this conversation at our next check in?

---

I've so appreciated this conversation. Let's revisit this after we've both had some time to consider. How's Tuesday?

---

I'd like some time to marinate. Shall I get back to you next week?

---

I want to give this the time it deserves. Let's hit pause here and decide on a time for our next discussion.

This will give you time to review your goals document (*Strategy 1: Identify Your Goals*) and check out how well the offer aligns with what you wanted when you were in a calm, intentional mindset. You'll be able to identify the easy wins or parts of the offer you're happy with, what you may want to negotiate, and what questions you want answered before you commit.

Timing your negotiation strategically can increase the likelihood of getting the response you want and prevent your next negotiation from feeling like a game of Red Light/Green Light that's completely out of control.

# Strategy 7: Start with Easy Wins

When asked what prevents them from negotiating, some women say it's a fear of damaging the relationship.[13]

Negotiation doesn't have to be adversarial! With the right mindset, it can be quite the opposite. The authors of *Getting to Yes* encourage counterparts in a negotiation to "sit on the same side of the table." They also use another analogy: instead of two attorneys battling it out in front of a jury, imagine judges working together on a joint opinion.[14]

When negotiating a new position, the process can actually enhance your relationship with your employer. It's an opportunity to demonstrate that you can professionally navigate a potentially challenging workplace situation.

Once you have an offer, you also have a shared goal: both you and your employer want you in this new role. At this point, it becomes a matter of figuring out how to make it mutually beneficial. If you compare the offer letter to what you wanted prior to the negotiation, you are likely to have several areas that you already agree on. Start with the easy wins.

## ☼ JOINING THE TEAM

Several years ago, I'd just started my consulting practice when a friend I'd previously worked with offered me a full-time leadership role at the nonprofit she led. I felt conflicted. On one hand, it was hard to pass up consistent income and the opportunity to contribute to an organization doing meaningful work. On the other hand, I didn't want to sacrifice the consulting practice I'd worked to build.

My friend told me, "I'll hire you as a consultant, or you can join the organization." Knowing I'm a huge nerd for collaboration and teamwork, she concluded her pitch to me with a brilliant line: "You just have to decide if you want to be on the team." My friend made it clear that she wanted to work with me, and having worked with her previously, I knew I wanted to work with her again. Once we had that shared goal in mind, it was just a matter of sorting out the logistics.

Going back to *Strategy 1: Define Your Goals*, I saw this position as a way to build out my consulting business while having stability and doing work that mattered to me.

Getting more specific, I wanted consistent income, flexibility to work with consulting clients, and to be clear this was a short-term role. A like-to-have for me was health insurance. In terms of her interests, my boss-friend was concerned about me staying in the loop, so she wanted to ensure I had face-time in the office and would attend all necessary meetings.

We started with the easy win, since we both knew we wanted me to take this role in some form. Then, we worked collaboratively to develop a six-month contract with me in the office three days, typically Mondays, Tuesdays, and Thursdays. I agreed to keep my shared calendar up to date and consistently attend staff meetings.

Since the health insurance policy required me to work 30 hours a week to receive coverage, that became the deciding factor. I joined the team with a flexible schedule, a 30-hour work week, and health benefits, all at a slightly lower salary than my boss-friend had budgeted for the full-time role.

It worked out beautifully for both my boss-friend and for me. In hiring me part-time, she was able to bring someone on board who could reliably run the department at a lower cost. I built out my consulting practice with the security of steady cash flow, the fulfillment of working on a cause that matters to me, and the joy of being on a team.

Because we began the conversation focused on our shared goals and easy wins, the other aspects of the negotiation were easier to determine collaboratively.

# Strategy 8: Ask Questions

Take a page out of every five-year-old's playbook. Imagine the kiddo who responds to an outcome they don't like or feel is unfair by whining, "But whyyyyy?" ad nauseum.

While I don't generally recommend behaving like a child, the impulse to understand more and more (and more) about your counterpart's goals and motivations is a good one. You'll remember that in a negotiation, people usually only communicate their position or desired outcome, rather than their interests.

As Rachel Krol, clinical instructor at the Harvard Negotiation & Mediation Clinical Program, explains, "A position is one possible agreement that is often presented in a negotiation as the only possible agreement. Rather than focusing on *what* they want, it's more important to understand *why* they want it. When negotiations focus on positions, they can stall or leave value on the table."

Krol suggests trying to understand your counterpart's underlying interests by asking yourself, "Why are they demanding that outcome? How does it help further their goals or protect them from risk?" She says, "Once you have a better understanding of their motivations and priorities, you can broaden the conversation to brainstorm other options that might work—both for them and for you."[15]

You can ask "What's your theory?" kinds of questions like "How did you arrive at that decision?" and "Why is that important to you?"

These open-ended questions can help tease out your counterpart's thought process, so you go from talking about positions to discussing interests.

Asking good questions can also help you get past those moments when you're at a standstill in a negotiation with your boss, partner, or airline customer service rep. A well-timed question is perfect for those moments when, explicitly or not, your counterpart is saying, "There's nothing more I can do," or "This conversation is over," but you're not ready to throw in the towel.

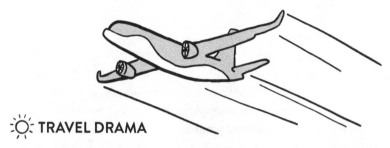

## ☼ TRAVEL DRAMA

In my travels as a speaker, I've hit many such roadblocks. One week, I was booked on a total of 16 flights trying to fly to and from just two (two!) client events. Due to weather delays, unrealistically tight connections, and a particularly embarrassing personal first (waking up 30 minutes after my ridiculously early morning flight departed), I found myself negotiating with many an airline employee.

At multiple points I heard things no business traveler wants to hear: there was no way I'd make it to my client event, and on one of the return trips, that there was no way for me to get home until after 1 am. I used open-ended questions as a way to facilitate empathy and get the negotiations unstuck.

In any negotiation, those dead ends tend to stem from each person being limited to their own perspective. Initially, my gate agents weren't getting creative. They understandably didn't see alternatives outside the process they were trained to use.

> The single question I've found to be most effective when I'm at this kind of impasse is, "What would you do if you were me?"

In my situation, I wanted to transition the conversation from our initial perspectives and take it from "I'm trying to get something from you, and you're following protocol" to "What would you do if you were in this situation?" For instance, on my way to Tampa, the connection through Atlanta was close to oversold. By asking employees what they would do in my situation, I learned that if I flew through Baltimore, I had a much better chance of getting a standby seat.

Travel Tetris aside, this question facilitates empathy by asking your counterpart to see the situation from your perspective. It gets them out of their default process or line of thinking, which is centered on their own vantage point.

Remember *Strategy 3: Do A Little Detective Work to Get to Know Your Counterpart.* Practicing empathy can provide a unique advantage, particularly when you're frustrated. Ask yourself what it feels like for your counterpart in this situation. Whether your boss is telling you that you didn't get the promotion, or the gate agent is telling you about yet another delay, they probably aren't thrilled to be the messenger.

Demonstrating empathy during a potentially adversarial conversation will help you to first be a kinder human, and second to enlist your counterpart's help as an ally.

## Learning from Rejection

Pretend for a moment that you've just been turned down for a promotion. Recognize whatever emotions come up for you. Sit with them. And whether you use journaling, therapy, or your favorite Jane Fonda exercise video, make it a point to work through those emotions when you're outside the office. Once you're ready to take the next step, try enlisting your boss or HR manager's help in achieving your goal.

You could say something like, "I really want to stay at [company name], and I want to advance in my career. Would you help me evaluate how that could look and what the steps are to get there? What would you do if you were me?"

This may give you fantastic new information. For example, it could prompt your decision-maker to share the evaluation process used to determine whether employees are ready for the next promotion, or your boss might end up helping you identify the skill set that you most need to improve.

No matter the situation, your counterpart will have their own perspective and different information than you do. Inevitably, this person will know things you don't know. Asking open-ended questions can help you evoke empathy and reach creative solutions.

In my own travel experience, through asking questions, using empathy, and creative problem solving, I made it to my client event with time to spare, and a few nights later, arrived home before midnight.

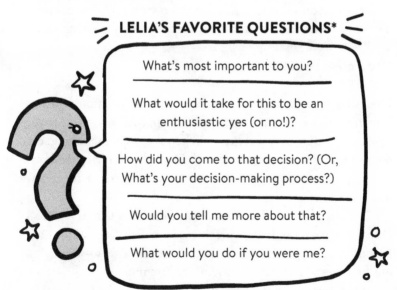

### LELIA'S FAVORITE QUESTIONS*

What's most important to you?

What would it take for this to be an enthusiastic yes (or no!)?

How did you come to that decision? (Or, What's your decision-making process?)

Would you tell me more about that?

What would you do if you were me?

*For a full list, check out the Negotiation Tooklit at www.negotiationfun.com/bonus

# Strategy 9: Listen

I am absolutely horrible at remembering people's names. Moments after an introduction, when someone has *just* said their name, I've already lost it. If I go back and try to remember the introduction, it goes something like this:

Me: Hi, I'm Lelia.

Mystery person: Hi, I'm [beeeeeeeeeep].

This has become such a frustrating problem that I've researched ways to improve. (They haven't worked.) But I did learn that one reason it's difficult to remember names when meeting new people is that we're so focused on making a good impression that we forget to listen. Psychologists call this the "next-in-line effect."[16] I'm so busy planning what to say next that I forget to listen.

This happens often in negotiation. You can be so worried about what you want to say or how to respond to your counterpart's last point that you don't consider what they're saying.

## Use Active Listening

One way to overcome this potential pitfall is through active listening. Active listening means giving your full attention to the speaker to ensure they feel heard. When they talk, make good eye contact and give the occasional nod. Once they finish, paraphrase or ask questions about what they've said *before* you make a new statement.

Take the brunch time banter on *Sex and the City* as a perfect example of what not to do when it comes to listening. While their friendships stuck it out over 94 episodes and two so-so movies, our heroines were positively terrible at listening.

They were always talking *at* one another, trading stories like a word association game. Charlotte mentions something that happened on Tuesday's dinner date, which is peripherally relevant

## ACTIVE LISTENING IN ACTION

"Am I understanding correctly that your biggest concern is about our billable hours this month?"

---

"It sounds like there's no way to improve the financial package associated with this offer. Is that right?"

---

"It's Marigny? What a beautiful name. How is that spelled?"

---

to Carrie's latest tryst, which reminds Miranda of this guy she used to date, which prompts Samantha to share her latest sexual conquest in detail. Rinse. Repeat. The conversation shifted focus constantly. It may make for compelling television, but its real-life corollary prevents the listener from feeling heard and hinders meaningful conversation.

In contrast, using active listening can slow down the conversation. It wouldn't play as well on TV, but it forces you to pay attention, shows you're invested in understanding your counterpart's side, and minimizes the risk of misunderstanding.

## Use Silence

As you strive to master active listening, don't underestimate the power of silence. For me, this is the most challenging aspect of listening. When I'm nervous I tend to speak more quickly—not exactly a helpful strategy in negotiation.

When I quoted my first fee, I told the client the price and didn't pause for a nanosecond before adding, "But of course I can discount it." You can avoid this mistake!

When you make a request or ask a question, do it and drop the mic. Be prepared to have uncomfortable silence, even if it means singing the ABCs in your head until your counterpart replies. If you keep talking, it lets them off the hook for responding to what you've said. Use silence to prompt your counterpart to speak. As the authors write in *Getting to Yes,* "Some of the most effective negotiating you will ever do is when you're not talking."[17]

In your next negotiation, try a combination of active listening and strategic silence. It'll help you remember to pay attention, ensure your counterpart feels heard, and make you a more successful negotiator.

# Strategy 10: Expand the Pie

The final strategy to employ during the negotiation is based on the "myth of the fixed pie." Imagine that pie is the total of what's available to be divided among the negotiators. There's a finite amount of pie, so if I eat a piece, that's one fewer piece you can have. In negotiation (and perhaps in real life), we want to make a bigger pie.

Consider this example. Charmaine is a scientist and Kristen is a chef, both of whom are travelling to a farm to buy rare plants. A finite number of plants are available, and Charmaine and Kristen each hope to purchase all the plants.

As seatmates on a long flight (what a coincidence!), they have ample time to discuss. Through open conversation and asking questions, the pair realizes that Charmaine the scientist wants to study a chemical compound found in the plants' roots for a vaccine she's developing, but Chef Kristen only needs the plants' leaves, which are used for food coloring.

Initially, both Charmaine's and Kristen's *positions* are, "I want to buy all of the available plants," but Charmaine's underlying *interest* is to make vaccines, for which she needs the plant root, while Kristen's *interest* is to make brilliantly colored designer macarons using the plant leaves.

Notice how expanding the pie often means increasing the number of variables and levers you can adjust. Whereas initially

Charmaine and Kristen's negotiation focused on the finite number of plants available for purchase, the negotiation quickly changed when they expanded the conversation to focus on the plant roots and leaves.

Expanding the pie in this way brings you beyond your counterpart's position so you can get to a deeper (and more interesting) conversation about interests. Both Charmaine and Kristen could leave the farm with the maximum amount of what they were looking for. Everyone wins!

| PERSPECTIVE | POSITION | INTEREST |
|---|---|---|
| Charmaine the scientist | I want to buy all the plants. | I want to make vaccines. (This requires the plant roots.) |
| Chef Kristen | I want to buy all the plants. | I want to make food coloring. (This requires the plant leaves.) |

## CONFERENCE PIE

When a nonprofit conference planner asked me to give a brief talk on negotiation, she told me right away that they didn't have the budget to pay my full speaker fee. After telling me about the conference and getting me excited about the audience, she said, "Are there non-monetary benefits that we can provide you? We want to make sure this is as beneficial to you as possible."

The question immediately changed the conversation from a single-issue negotiation, focused on money in exchange for one speech, to a conversation focused on expanding the metaphorical pie. We were no longer stuck in our positions, where we'd reached an impasse: I wanted her to pay my full speaker fee and she wasn't able to pay it. Instead, by discussing our interests, we were sitting on the same side of the table and creatively solving a problem together.

At the time, my primary interests were to receive fair pay, work with an audience that energizes me, and secure future gigs. Her interests were to stay within budget, build relationships with quality local speakers, and host a phenomenal event.

After a few minutes of brainstorming, I agreed to give the talk, and she agreed to:

- Record the speech
- Pay me to speak at another event in the future at my full rate
- Promote my content on social media
- Provide a testimonial after the event
- Refer other clients to me

In this case, my client initiated the pie expansion, but either party can start the conversation and help reach a creative, mutually beneficial agreement. Bonus points if you're the one who gets the ball rolling in that direction, since you'll demonstrate empathy and concern for your counterpart.

## REFLECTION QUESTIONS

- In your opinion, which would be worse, a negotiation that starts before you're ready or one that just won't end?
- What do you want your go-to Red Light Phrase to be?
- When was the last time you wish you had used silence as a negotiating tactic?
- What's your favorite kind of pie? Do you think bringing an actual pie to your next negotiation will help?

# NOTES!

# Part Four

# PERSPECTIVE

---

Strategies for Navigating

Your Emotions

The advice "Never bring your emotions into a negotiation" is as common as it is crappy and unrealistic.

Many of us spend the majority of our waking hours working, so the negotiations we have about our jobs significantly impact our quality of life. Of course, we have some feelings about them.

Building from a client's real-life scenario, imagine for a moment that your boss casually references the possibility of a major promotion. In that same conversation, your boss also asks you to take on a new project that's outside of your current purview. You might feel:

- **Nervous** about how your performance on this project could impact the promotion
- **Excited** about the possibility of a new role
- **Uncertain** about how much work to do in this new capacity before advocating for the promotion
- **Fearful** of damaging the relationship if you do advocate for yourself
- **Stressed** about how you'll balance the new responsibilities
- **Hopeful** about the increased salary from the promotion
- **Hesitant** about whether you even want the promotion at all
- **Presumptuous** for thinking so much about a job that doesn't even exist yet

You may swing through a wide range of emotions or experience seemingly contradictory feelings simultaneously. This is all NORMAL.*

Furthermore, for a lot of us, our work is a key part of our identities. When I negotiated with Cecilia and accepted a low

---

* When I taught sex education to fifth-graders, it was important to me to normalize their questions about sexuality and their bodies. I may have overshot the mark. I said "That's ok. That's normal," so often that the students started teasing me, repeating it playfully until it effectively became my catchphrase.

rate to be published in the fancy publication, I recognized self-doubt creeping into my negotiation. I found myself wondering whether a "real" writer would have gotten paid more. While these thoughts may be unpleasant, again, they're normal.

Y'all, I'd be worried if we *didn't* have emotions about the negotiations surrounding our careers.

In my experience with clients, a lot of the work surrounding negotiation involves learning to recognize and work through the emotions that come up during the process rather than trying to push them away.

## Trust Me, I'm an Expert

When I was in high school, my classmates and I used the expression "I feel yucky" as a catch-all for any unpleasant emotion. It captured everything from "I'm terrified I bombed the geometry test," to "I'm nervous I'll run into my ex between classes," to "I'm hangry, and I don't have a snack." I said, "I feel yucky" with such frequency that a friend gave me a visor embroidered with the word "yucky" as a birthday present. (I felt very seen.)

In hindsight, this was a coping mechanism. Describing all my negative feels as "yucky" was the perfect way to avoid having to meaningfully explore or grapple with my emotions.

As a grown-ass woman, I realize feelings don't fit neatly into two binary categories, pleasant ones to seek out and "yucky" ones to avoid. Having benefited from coaching and therapy, I now strive to name and accept my feelings, even the "yucky" ones, as they arise.

As my phenomenal coach, psychologist Tim Kershenstine, told me, "Emotions, like waves in the ocean, will be there and continuously change. Learn to surf the waves of emotions, as opposed to the futile effort to control or change them."

When we've had years of experience connecting negotiation with negative emotions, we can default to our typical response and spiral into feeling "yucky" when we see a negotiation coming.

Rather than trying to "should" yourself into having the feelings you would prefer to have or think you're supposed to have, strive to sit with your discomfort. It can be challenging, but you can do it. Practice saying, "I am just going to name this emotion I'm experiencing right now. I'm feeling [insert emotion here]. That's ok. I won't feel this way forever."

Tom Drummond's *Vocabulary of Emotions* (included in the online Negotiation Toolkit www.negotiationfun.com/bonus) can be a powerful resource for getting more specific about what's coming up for you. Next time you feel "yucky," Drummond's list can help you navigate what's really going on. Perhaps you're feeling incompetent, panicky, or disconcerted. Articulating those more nuanced emotions can help you accept and move through them. And when you can do that, you can show up to any negotiation with clarity and confidence.

The authors of the book *Difficult Conversations* write, "It doesn't matter if your feelings are reasonable or rational. What matters is that they're there... Feelings are too powerful to remain peacefully bottled. They will be heard one way or another, whether in leaks or bursts."[18] The goal is to recognize and acknowledge them, releasing them as they happen, rather than having them burst out unexpectedly, soaking everyone with All. The. Feels.

A note about timing: Consider how you can hold space for your feelings before and after the negotiation. That way, you can be fully present and focused when you're in the midst of a discussion aimed at reaching an agreement.

If you find yourself confronted with a wave of emotion that feels unmanageable during your negotiation, remember *Strategy 6: Time Your Negotiation Strategically.* There's absolutely no shame in asking to take a break or to reconnect at a later date.

I get real fired up about this. All of my clients' most significant negotiation "wins" can be attributed in large part to them finding clarity about their goals, becoming aware of their emotions around the negotiation at hand, and working through them. The following tools will help you tap into your emotions and navigate them effectively throughout the negotiation process.

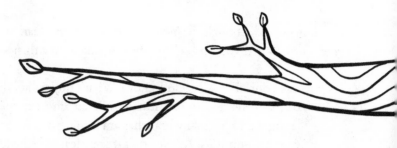

# Strategy 11: Maintain Perspective and Keep Branch Walking to a Minimum

After graduating from her master's program, a client was having a difficult time finding a job in her field. Whenever she got stressed (which was often), she'd tell herself, "What if I don't find a job, go through my savings, and can't pay my rent—then who knows what will happen."

I call this nightmarish game of what ifs, imagining the very worst thing that could happen and assuming that's the likeliest outcome, "branch walking."[19] Envision the trunk of the tree as reality. Each time you say, "what if," you're walking onto a new branch.

As you move farther from the trunk of the tree, the branches get thinner. Your footing is less stable, and you're likely to get more frantic as your precarious game of what ifs becomes more and more dangerous.

Instead of walking further out on those twigs, recognize that you're only walking on fears and doubts based largely on speculation. As a lovely data nerd in one of my talks shared, each time you walk out on a new branch, you're envisioning a statistically less probable outcome.

On occasion, it can actually be healthy to catastrophize on purpose, to branch walk until you get to that final twig on the last branch and say, "Ok, this is pretty unlikely and the very worst case scenario, but I could probably deal with it if it happens."

Unchecked, though, branch walking can cause fear, anxiety, and stress. When you find self-doubt creeping in, try this:

1. Ask yourself, "What do I know? What's the reality, the trunk of the tree, in my situation? What am I extrapolating, and how many branches am I going out?" Test your assumptions. Ask yourself if your fear is realistic or an unlikely worst-case scenario. If you're stuck in your own head, it can be hard to evaluate your circumstances rationally, so this is a great time to ask a trusted friend or advisor for help evaluating the situation. When I'm stressed and spiraling, my best friend now uses my favorite terminology with me, asking, "Do you think maybe you're branch walking?"

2. If your branch walking involves another person, employ *Strategy 8: Ask Questions* and strive to ask them open-ended questions. For instance, if you think your boss is pissed about the way you're handling a new project, rather than saying, "It seems like you're mad at me," give them an opportunity to share their experience without getting defensive.

3. You could ask, "From your perspective, how are things going on the new project?" That way, you're asking questions that promote a dialogue rather than listening to the monologue of self-doubt playing on a loop in your head.

The apocalyptic situation my client envisioned when branch walking did not come to fruition. She ended up living with family and taking a few crappy short-term jobs to make ends meet, but things worked out. Though she may not have taken her ideal path to get there, ultimately, she landed a great job in her field.

## Keep Perspective

In a commonly referenced cartoon in the literature on professional confidence for women, a woman and a man are each putting on a pair of pants that is too small. The woman's thought bubble says, "I must be gaining weight." The man's says, "There must be something wrong with these pants."

Sound familiar? As women, to a much greater degree than men, we take responsibility in situations that are out of our control.[20] We tend to internalize a lack of information and assume something negative, taking responsibility for something even though *it may not have had a damn thing to do with us.*

Something bad happened! Must be our fault.

Someone didn't call us back! They must be mad at us.

It's a classic form of branch walking: we interpret a situation that exists independently of us as feedback and imagine the worst-case scenario.

## ☀ SILENCE IS DECIDEDLY NOT GOLDEN

Back when I was a Jacklyn of all trades, one of my roles was to work with teachers and principals on education policy. I provided feedback on educators' op-eds and helped them navigate the submission process, deciding which publications to pitch and when and how long to wait before submitting the pieces elsewhere.

When an educator with whom I'd worked closely didn't hear back from her first-choice media outlet, she concluded that her op-ed must not have been good and attributed her previous publishing success to "beginner's luck." Surely, she'd never be published again. It was textbook branch walking. She was ready to give up, taking responsibility for the lack of response from the editor.

I pulled her back to the trunk of the tree and asked, "What do we know?" We knew:

- The newspaper industry was on life support, and journalists and editors were regularly laid off, leaving the remaining editors with an enormous workload.
- This paper had published one of her op-eds in the last three months, and papers don't tend to want to highlight the same voices repeatedly.
- My job was to help get op-eds published, and I was confident that it was a particularly good one, worthy of publication.

While she never heard back from that first publisher, she ultimately resubmitted and got the piece published in a different news outlet. Since then, she's continued writing op-eds and guest columns.

## Putting It into Action

Pretend for a moment that you've been asked to take on your first project as an independent consultant. You invest significant energy in crafting the proposal and finally send it out after several rounds of feedback and revisions. You nervously await a reply. One week goes by and then another. What might branch walking sound like as you wait for a reply?

You might fear that you're out of your league professionally. You might worry that your fee was too high. You might imagine your client laughing at your proposal and you.

Interrupting these thoughts is far easier when you've got a friend to help put things in context. Here's how a friend could help.

**Friend: What are you assuming?**
You: The client thinks I asked for too much and I'm unqualified. They're mad at me.

**Friend: Why do you assume that?**
You: Because I haven't gotten an email response.

**Friend: What else have they done that makes you think they're unhappy?**
You: Nothing. Ahh, I see what you're doing here. I have no other reasons.

**Friend: Ok, so what other conclusions could you draw from this data?**
You: My client is on vacation, in the hospital, or is selling my awesome proposal to her boss. Oh!

Rather than branch walking and becoming consumed with fearful scenarios until you hear back, enlist the help of a rational friend so you can keep perspective.

# Strategy 12: Practice Self-Compassion for Fun and Profit

Sometimes, despite our best efforts, our negotiations don't go the way we'd like. And then what? Well, we might start thinking that every future negotiation will fall apart, result in a no, or be a torturous, unsuccessful misery fest.

Bizarre as it sounds, there's good reason our minds jump to the worst-case scenario. Human brains are wired to remember negative experiences more than the positive ones. Scientists refer to this as "negativity bias."[21] For our ancestors, survival depended on remembering negative information like "There are bears in that cave!" By comparison, positive or neutral info like "That hill is a great place to watch the sunset," was dandy, but not a priority for our subconscious.

Today, bad negotiations are like bears. We remember them in detail because in the future, our brains want to protect us from these "dangerous" situations. Like sunsets, positive or neutral experiences are less memorable because our brains don't see them as a priority.

But hopefully, a bad negotiation won't kill us. So, how can we move forward? Since our brains don't come with an override feature for negativity bias or self-doubt, we're going to use self-compassion.

It's a surprisingly powerful tool. Psychologist Kristin Neff's research found that self-compassion improves emotional resilience.[23] Basically, using Neff's three strategies to be nicer to yourself will help you bounce back from failure and other challenging experiences.

## ☀ DREAM CLIENT NIGHTMARE

When I first started my business, I had to navigate a situation that was far more bear than sunset. In retrospect, I would've benefited from a massive dose of self-compassion.

Over seven months, I diligently cultivated what was going to be my largest contract to date: a yearlong goal-setting program for a well-funded professional association.

The women I met through the planning process were total badasses, achieving professional success within a male-dominated industry. Over lunch, they talked about how much it pissed them off to be told to act like men to be successful and traded horror stories about golf tournaments gone wrong. Frankly, I felt really cool that they wanted to work with me, and the organization was an ideal client.

After numerous phone conferences and in-person meetings, we negotiated a scope of work that would provide them with great content and bring me considerable financial stability. I wrote a contract and waited for them to sign. And waited.

Months of excruciating correspondence followed. Their attorney had some edits. Their contact person changed. Eventually, they told me their professional development budget had been cut. I reluctantly agreed to pare down the project to a tenth of what we'd initially agreed to, and then they ghosted me completely.

Afterwards, my inner monologue channeled Meryl Streep's character in *The Devil Wears Prada*. For those of you who haven't had the pleasure, Streep's communication style in the film is best represented by such gems as, "Details of your incompetence do not interest me." I berated myself with biting comments and a dismissive, judgmental tone.

Below, I'll share what those critical thoughts sounded like in real time and take us through what Neff's three strategies for self-compassion would have sounded like instead.

## 1. Self-kindness (vs. Self-judgment)

Author Mike Robbins says, "We get training on how to interact with others, but we don't get much training on how to interact with ourselves."[24] If you've ever written out your inner monologue when you're most frustrated with yourself, odds are pretty good you're saying things to yourself you'd never say to another person, let alone someone you cared about.

To apply self-kindness, speak to yourself the same way you'd talk to a beloved friend. Rather than jumping to *The Devil Wears Prada*-style judgment, strive to be caring and understanding with yourself. Use a tone that's comforting and soothing. Neff suggests, "May I give myself the compassion that I need."

Self-compassion means seeing our flaws as a normal part of who we are. Neff writes, "Rather than relentlessly criticizing ourselves for being inadequate, self-compassion means accepting the fact that we are imperfect."

Here's a replay of my inner monologue after my meeting using the two different approaches:

**Self-judgment:** "Who the hell did you think you were, anyway? These women have far more experience and gravitas than you do. It's cute that you thought *you* could help *them*. Sure, their budget was cut, but if you were good at what you do, they would've found a way to hire you. Once they figured out you are a total newbie, they couldn't even be bothered to follow up."

**Self-kindness:** "This was a hard one. You really liked these women, and it's painful to have that relationship sour. Notice the emotions that are coming up and be careful about branch walking. This may have nothing to do with you. If you want to learn from the experience, perhaps you could have set clearer timelines up front. You can't redo it now, though, and that's ok. Not every contract is going to go perfectly. Be gentle with yourself."

## 2. A Sense of Common Humanity (vs. A Sense of Isolation)

When we struggle or make a mistake, we often think, "There's something wrong with me," or judge ourselves as fundamentally flawed. Our failure or heartache becomes something we need to hide or push through. Instead, Neff encourages people to embrace these flaws as an indication of our humanity.

Everyone has insecurities, screws up, and experiences failure, even the people who impress us most. Again, it's super normal. Others have felt the emotions you're feeling. The context may be unique, but the emotions are universal.

Here's the replay:

**Sense of isolation:** "Oh, you screwed up big time and you should be seriously embarrassed. You got your hopes up and fell flat on your face because you have no idea what you're doing. A real entrepreneur would have navigated the timeline more efficiently and landed the contract."

**Sense of common humanity:** "Hey, guess what? This kind of thing happens to *everyone*. Think about your friend who bombed his job interview after several friends had recommended him for the role. He felt so out of his league, he was mortified he'd even applied. But he didn't combust from shame. A few years later, he even landed a gig overseeing interviews and hiring for that same organization. Mistakes and failures are a totally normal (and in fairness, a kind of sucky) part of being human."

### 3. Mindfulness (vs. Over-identification)

When I'm upset, I tend to obsess on the most embarrassing, stressful, or problematic aspects of the situation and assume I'll feel the way I feel now, forever. When we fixate on our flaws or current circumstances and can't see beyond them, Neff calls this "over-identification."

Practicing mindfulness, on the other hand, allows us to approach these situations with valuable perspective as we consider the moment in a larger context. It provides greater objectivity.

One phrase Neff suggests has been particularly resonant to me: "This is a moment of suffering." It helps me tap into perspective (this is just the present moment) and awareness (this hurts). It reminds me that I can experience challenging emotions safely without being totally wrecked by them forever and ever.

Here's the replay:

**Over-identification:** "Clearly, this business is totally unrealistic, and there's no way it will be successful. I was counting on this revenue, and now I'm screwed, resentful, and stressed. They're probably laughing with their friends about how I'm out of my league. I'm mortified. I wonder what other clients are about to drop me."

**Mindfulness:** "Ouch. I notice I'm experiencing a lot of emotions about this particular client relationship, which didn't go as I had hoped. In the past, I've developed beautiful, impactful relationships with my clients. While my feelings in this moment are valid, they will change. How I feel in this moment is not how I will feel forever."

I offer self-compassion as a penultimate strategy to reframe negotiation because even with all of your strengths and new negotiation skills, setbacks are inevitable. I spend much of my time teaching this stuff, and on occasion, I still bomb negotiations (see above).

I find that when I'm working hard to get everything "just right," I tend to beat myself up, becoming frozen by perfectionism. So, instead, I strive for imperfect action. Likewise, the goal here isn't for you to perfectly execute each of these strategies in every negotiation. Instead, it's that you explore these strategies and find your own negotiation voice.

Self-compassion is an imperative part of that process.

Next time you find yourself anxious about negotiation or your self-esteem is shaken, try this: give yourself five minutes to write down all of the stresses, worries, and nasty thoughts coming up in your mind. Take three big breaths to reset. Then reassess the situation using the three strategies of self-compassion: self-kindness, a sense of common humanity, and mindfulness.

**It might not be easy at first, but like most things, the more you practice self-compassion, the easier it becomes.**

Years after the above scenario, and just weeks before this book went to print, new leadership at the professional association that ghosted me reached out. They wanted to hire me to give the keynote for an event. Full circle!

# Strategy 13: Play to Your Strengths and Try It On

"What will happen when we think about what's right with people rather than fixating on what's wrong with them?"

That is the question my colleague and dear friend Marta Hanson asks as a certified Gallup strengths coach.

Typically, she says, we focus on being well-rounded and prioritize efforts to improve our weaknesses. Instead, her strengths-based approach encourages us to understand, invest in, and embrace our innate talents.

To explain, Hanson uses the metaphor of a star. A star has dips and points. When we focus on our weaknesses—the dips in our star—it's in service of becoming well-rounded. This creates average performance, and in place of the star, a smooth circle.

Alternatively, the strengths-based approach asks us to spend our finite time and energy sharpening our talents. In developing excellence in a few specific areas, we're aiming to create the biggest, sparkliest, and pointiest star possible.

The strengths-based approach is backed by decades of research that shows that people who actively use their strengths every day report higher quality of life, higher engagement at work, and higher productivity. [21] Similarly, when we tap into our strengths during negotiation, we see better results.

When it comes to finding your authentic negotiating voice, I think of my friend Jenny's cousin's therapist (of all people) who says, "try it on." Jenny explains: "When you're deciding what to wear, you try on several different things from *your* closet until you find an outfit that works. You don't try on my clothes, because they wouldn't fit you. The same principle applies to negotiation styles, career paths, etc."

In the context of a negotiation,
try on your various strengths
and aspects of your personality.
There's no right answer. Everyone's
star will look different, and your
strengths can show up differently
in different situations. Strive to
hold negotiation lightly so you can
explore what feels comfortable and
authentic for you.

**Using the list below to get you started, what strengths resonate most for you? What are the five points on your star?***

- Adaptable
- Analytical
- Appreciative
- Creative
- Courageous
- Curious
- Dedicated
- Deliberative
- Disciplined

- Empathetic
- Enthusiastic
- Fair
- Funny
- Honest
- Humble
- Inspiring
- Intuitive
- Kind

- Motivated
- Optimistic
- Passionate
- Patient
- Playful
- Self-aware
- Reliable
- Trustworthy
- Versatile

**Try It On!**

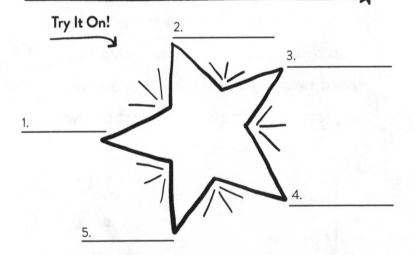

1.

2.

3.

4.

5.

*The Clifton StrengthsFinder assessment from Gallup can also be a great resource. The assessment asks you to put yourself on a continuum between pairs of self-descriptors, such as "I read instructions carefully" and "I like to jump right into things." After completing the assessment (which I think is pretty fun), you'll receive a Strengths Insight Report, which includes a framework to help you understand your top 5 strengths.

## REFLECTION QUESTIONS

- What's your most elaborate branch walk to date? What was its epic conclusion? In real life, was it as bad as you thought it would be?
- Think of a past negotiation in which you felt "yucky." What emotions came up for you? Would you navigate them differently if you could do it again?
- What are the points on your star? Which of your strengths serve you best in negotiations?

# Parting Words

No single personality trait makes for a good negotiator. Before you purchased this book, you already had many of the qualities and skills that make someone effective. This book is designed to help you recognize and tap into those strengths. The 13 strategies we've explored will further set you up for success.

One of my very first clients was extremely nervous about a negotiation with her prospective employer. The conversation didn't go as she had expected, but she still felt prepared. Using our strategies, she left happy with both the process and the outcome.

Her employer felt similarly. A few weeks after my client started her role, the HR director reached out. To paraphrase the conversation, she told my client, "I was impressed with how you handled the negotiation. Some people who don't negotiate end up resentful in three months. While we couldn't meet everything that you asked for, I'm glad you negotiated because I think you'll be happy here."

We're reclaiming negotiation as something that's personally rewarding *and* creates stronger relationships. In fact, we negotiate all the time, and we're already pretty damn good at it.

You are totally capable of rocking the socks off of your workplace negotiations on your terms. With these tools, you'll increase your impact and build a more fulfilling and profitable career.

YOU
GOT
THIS

# THE RUNDOWN

## NEGOTIATIONS AT A GLANCE

Let me know how it goes!
I'd love to stay in touch via my website
www.leliagowland.com and social media.
I'm @leliagowland most places.

# BEFORE THE NEGOTIATION

**1. Identify Your Goals:** By starting the negotiation with a clear written list of your priorities, you're less likely to be swayed by things that don't matter to you. When you don't get distracted by something shiny but unimportant— "Ooh, look at this corner office!"—you'll have better leverage to get the things that do matter.

**2. Do Your Research and Use Precedent to Your Advantage:** By grounding your proposal in data and research, you set realistic expectations, position yourself well within the negotiation, and increase the likelihood that you'll reach a fair offer. (You'll also sound like a smart, resourceful person.)

**3. Do a Little Detective Work to Get to Know Your Counterpart:** Build empathy for your counterpart by trying to understand their story, experiences, and motivations in advance of the negotiation. Use social media and the interwebs as tools for negotiation success. (Then, if you have time, maybe see what your middle school crush is up to.)

**4. Know Your Alternatives:** If you have a Plan B to compare with the agreement you're considering, you'll be better poised to recognize a good deal and walk away from a bad one. Know your options!

**5. Practice, Practice, Practice:** Avoid word vomit by practicing *out loud* what you'd like to communicate and how you'll reply to challenges. Remember the types of role-play: Silly to Serious, Nightmare Scenario, Realistic Scenario, and As Your Counterpart. If you're comfortable with your language, your approach to the negotiation will be far more compelling to your counterpart and easier for you.

## DURING THE NEGOTIATION

**6. Time the Negotiation Strategically:** Strive to be intentional about when you begin a negotiation and when it's advantageous to delay it. You just landed a big account? Strike now. Boss's divorce just finalized? Maybe give it time.

**7. Start with Easy Wins:** To build rapport, start with a mutually beneficial goal and identify the low hanging fruit. For example, in a job interview, the employer wants to hire someone, and you want to get hired. You have so much in common!

**8. Ask Questions:** Channel your inner five-year-old by asking tons of questions to increase empathy and learn more about your counterpart's goals.

**9. Listen:** Don't forget to listen! Active listening or paraphrasing what your counterpart says can help you remember to stay tuned and will demonstrate interest in your counterpart's perspective. "It sounds like you're saying X. If that's the case, then…" Also, don't forget to "zip it." Strategic silence can be a stellar advantage.

**10. Expand the Pie:** I like pie. You like pie. Let's make a bigger pie so we both get to have as much pie as possible. Do this by getting more specific about your interests and introducing more variables into the negotiation.

## AFTER THE NEGOTIATION

**11.  Maintain Perspective and Keep Branch Walking to a Minimum:** The what-if game can be exhausting, but it can be helpful to deliberately think of the worst outcome and recognize you could totally deal. Remember, though, when it comes to branch walking, the further from the tree, the less likely the result.

**12.  Practice Self-Compassion for Fun and Profit:** Pay attention to how you talk to yourself and strive to use mindfulness, a sense of common humanity, and self-kindness. Just because one negotiation didn't go as planned, that doesn't mean that you won't ace your next one.

**13.  Play to Your Strengths and Try It On:** Explore which strengths and aspects of your identity feel comfy and authentic. Remember, you already have a lot of the qualities of a successful negotiator.

### ☆ BONUS CONTENT! ☆ ·

Don't forget the bonus content waiting for you at www.negotiationfun.com/bonus! It includes the tools I use when I negotiate, your one-page Negotiation Cheat Sheet, and more. Oh, and the Ultimate Negotiation Playlist to get you fired up.

YOU GOT THIS!

# PREPARATION
## Strategies for Before You Negotiate

### 1. Identify Your Goals
- What is your position? (What's your desired outcome or the best way you can think to resolve the negotiation?)
- What is your interest? (What's your underlying goal or motivation?)

### 2. Research the Situation and Use Precedent to Your Advantage
- What do you know about the context of your negotiation?
- What could you find out?

### 3. Do a Little Detective Work to Get to Know Your Counterpart
- What do you know about your counterpart?
- What motivates them? How do they like to receive information?

### 4. Know Your Alternatives
- What are the alternatives if this negotiation doesn't pan out? Include "doing nothing" as an option.
- What's your Plan B (best single alternative)?

### 5. Practice, Practice, Practice
- Who can be your role play buddy?
- Is there specific language you'd like to practice?

# PRESENCE
## Strategies for During the Negotiation

### 6. Time Your Negotiation Strategically
- How will you know you're ready to start the negotiation?
- What are some Red Light Phrases you could use to stop the negotiation?

### 7. Start with Easy Wins
- Where is there already agreement?
- How can you sit on the same side of the table?

### 8. Ask Questions
- What questions do you have for your counterpart? (Come with at least 3.)
- What questions might they have for you?

### 9. Listen
- What active listening phrases do you like best? Ex: "What I'm hearing you say is… Is that right?"
- What song will you sing in your head to help you use silence as a tool?

### 10. Expand the Pie
- How can you make an agreement that's as mutually beneficial as possible?
- Can you think of 3 more variables you haven't considered?

# PERSPECTIVE
## Strategies for Navigating Your Emotions

### 11. Maintain Perspective and Keep Branch Walking to a Minimum
- Where can you get support?
- What tools or people can help bring you back to the trunk of the tree?

### 12. Practice Self-Compassion for Fun and Profit
- What do the following strategies sound like for you in this situation?
- Self-kindness (Ex: May I give myself the compassion that I need.)
- A sense of common humanity (Ex: Everything I'm feeling is normal.)
- Mindfulness (Ex: This is a moment of suffering.)

### 13. Play to Your Strengths and Try It On
- What are your strengths as a negotiator?
- How do you want to show up for this negotiation?

# ☆ NOTES! ☆

# Acknowledgements

In an ideal world, I'd write an effusive handwritten thank you note to each of the following people. I'd send it via the USPS (those folks don't get enough credit!) in an embossed envelope with a fun stamp. While I'm a snail mail enthusiast, I want to share my gratitude with all y'all and celebrate the wonderful people who made this book possible.

Throughout the writing process, I felt supported by a phenomenal team of clients, friends, and colleagues. Victoria Adams Phipps, Kara Cohen, Laura Cathcart Robbins, Dina de Veer Giannetta, Lydia Frank, Charlotte Gill, Anya Groner, Mallory Josol Corbin, Natalie Kaharick, Rachel Krol, Linette Lopez, Marie Elizabeth Oliver, Stephanie Powell, Rémy Robert, Ciji Townsend, Kelly Williams Brown—your encouragement, edits, and expertise were fundamental to bringing this book to fruition.

Sarah Edwards, in addition to being a gifted writer and editor, you are one of the most thoughtful and emotionally intelligent people I know. You regularly offer me new insight into my own thinking, both professionally and personally. This book is no exception. Thank you.

Lauren Cutuli, Jen Engquist, Shannon Garrety, Kate Naranjo, and Kara Peneguy, thank you for investing your time and skills in working with me. My business and this book are better for it.

Without the New Leaders Council (NLC), this book and my entire business might not have come into being. Specifically, thank you to Julie Barton, Clare Bresnahan English, Marta Hanson, Ryan James Evans, Lorena O'Neil, and my entire 2015 cohort. To all of my NLC family, I'm endlessly grateful for your encouragement and feedback on the business and this book. NLC changes lives, and I'm grateful to each of you for changing mine.

Finally, my family shows up for me again and again. Milly and Peter, our time together is always a powerful recharge. Sistra, thank you for being Auntie Colyn and for all the food and Fe QT.

Bryan, thank you for being my Best Man + Best Friend. No one could be more deserving of that title. Granny, at the end of each year when I reflect about what's been most meaningful, spending quality time with you always makes the top of the list.

Melissa, your posts and texts of encouragement mean more than you know. I'll always be Lilsis1385(@aol.com) and am forever grateful that you initiated my love of costuming. Baby Rock Bop forever.

Susan, you're the best Step-Monster a gal could ask for. Thank you for always reminding me that I can't expect people to respond to me the way I respond to them. Dad, I'm glad you allow me to put your laser editing eyes to such good use. Love you +1.

Mom, the optimism and affirming approach that you modeled for me is fundamental to how and why I do this work. Thank you for teaching me that it's important to love your work. Whether you're providing thoughtful late-night edits or celebrating each step with me, I feel so fortunate to have you in my corner.

Cole, you (almost always) know what I'm trying to say. While we disagree on sentence length, you make me a better writer and human. Come hell or high water, zombie apocalypse or dinosaur attack, I can't imagine a better co-parent or life partner. Thanks for doing life with me.

And to Felix (aka "Little Monster"), it's so fun to be your mom. May you be a feminist like your pop.

# References

1    Ann Friedman, "Astronaut Sally Ride and the Burden of Being The First," *The American Prospect*, June 19, 2014, http://prospect.org/article/astronaut-sally-ride-and-burden-being-first.

2    Linda Babcock and Sara Laschever, *Women Don't Ask: The High Cost of Avoiding Negotiation-and Positive Strategies for Change* (Bantam Dell, 2007), 125.

3    Babcock and Laschever, *Women Don't Ask*, 125.

4    Babcock and Laschever, *Women Don't Ask*, 4.

5    Hannah Riley Bowles, "Psychological Perspectives on Gender in Negotiation," *The Sage Handbook of Gender and Psychology*, 2013, 465–483.

6    Shira Mor et al., "Iron Fist in a Velvet Glove: Gender/Professional Identity Integration Promotes Women's Negotiation Performance," SSRN Scholarly Paper (Rochester, NY: Social Science Research Network, February 21, 2014), https://papers.ssrn.com/abstract=2451067.

7    Babcock and Laschever, *Women Don't Ask*.

8    Janet W. Hardy and Dossie Easton, *The Ethical Slut: A Practical Guide to Polyamory, Open Relationships, and Other Freedoms in Sex and Love*, 3rd ed. (Ten Speed Press, 2017).

9    Sally Krawcheck, *Own It* (New York: Crown Business, 2017), 79.

10   "Women in the Workplace 2016 | McKinsey," accessed June 5, 2017, https://www.mckinsey.com/business-functions/organization/our-insights/women-in-the-workplace-2016.

11   Roger Fisher, William Ury, and Bruce Patton, *Getting to Yes: Negotiating Agreement Without Giving In*, Second Edition (Penguin Group, 1991), 100.

12   "Salary History Stats and Infographics | PayScale," accessed June 12, 2018, https://www.payscale.com/data/salary-history.

13   Babcock and Laschever, *Women Don't Ask*.

14   Fisher, Ury, and Patton, *Getting to Yes*, 35.

15   "Next-in-Line Effect - Oxford Reference," accessed September 1, 2017, http://www.oxfordreference.com/view/10.1093/oi/authority.20110803100232913.

16   Rachel Krol, Google Drive comment to the author, August 17, 2017.

17   Fisher, Ury, and Patton, *Getting to Yes*, 112.

18   Douglas Stone, Bruce Patton, and Sheila Heen, *Difficult Conversations* (New York: Viking, 1999), 97 and 85.

19   A brilliant term created by my friend's father, Reed Eckhardt.

20   Babcock and Laschever, *Women Don't Ask*.

21   Emma Seppälä, *The Happiness Track: How to Apply the Science of Happiness to Accelerate Your Success* (New York: HarperCollins, 2016).

22   "Learn How the CliftonStrengths Assessment Works | Gallup," accessed August 21, 2018, https://www.gallupstrengthscenter.com/home/en-us/about.

23   Kristin D. Neff, "Self-Compassion, Self-Esteem, and Well-Being: Self-Compassion, Self-Esteem, and Well-Being," *Social and Personality Psychology Compass* 5, no. 1 (January 2011): 1–12, https://doi.org/10.1111/j.1751-9004.2010.00330.x.

24   Mike Robbins, "Nothing Changes Until You Do" (Presentation at the Self-Acceptance Summit, virtual conference, September 15, 2017).

# Bibliography

Babcock, Linda, and Sara Laschever. *Women Don't Ask: The High Cost of Avoiding Negotiation-and Positive Strategies for Change*. Bantam Dell, 2007.

Bowles, Hannah Riley. "Psychological Perspectives on Gender in Negotiation." *The Sage Handbook of Gender and Psychology*, 2013, 465–483.

Fisher, Roger, William Ury, and Bruce Patton. *Getting to Yes: Negotiating Agreement Without Giving In*. Second Edition. Penguin Group, 1991.

Friedman, Ann. "Astronaut Sally Ride and the Burden of Being The First." *The American Prospect*, June 19, 2014. http://prospect.org/article/astronaut-sally-ride-and-burden-being-first.

Hardy, Janet W. and Dossie Easton. *The Ethical Slut: A Practical Guide to Polyamory, Open Relationships, and Other Freedoms in Sex and Love,* 3rd ed. Ten Speed Press, 2017.

Krawcheck, Sally. *Own It*. New York: Crown Business, 2017.

"Learn How the CliftonStrengths Assessment Works | Gallup." Accessed September 5, 2019. https://www.gallupstrengthscenter.com/home/en-us/about.

Mor, Shira, Pranjal Mehta, Ilona Fridman, and Michael Morris. "Iron Fist in a Velvet Glove: Gender/Professional Identity Integration Promotes Women's Negotiation Performance." SSRN Scholarly Paper. Rochester, NY: Social Science Research Network, February 21, 2014.

Neff, Kristin D. "Self-Compassion, Self-Esteem, and Well-Being: Self-Compassion, Self-Esteem, and Well-Being." *Social and Personality Psychology Compass 5*, no. 1, January 2011, 1–12.

"Next-in-Line Effect - Oxford Reference." Accessed September 1, 2017. http://www.oxfordreference.com/view/10.1093/oi/authority.20110803100232913.

Robbins, Mike. "Nothing Changes Until You Do." Presentation at the Self-Acceptance Summit, virtual conference, September 15, 2017.

"Salary History Stats and Infographics | PayScale." Accessed September 5, 2019. https://www.payscale.com/data/salary-history.

Seppälä, Emma. *The Happiness Track: How to Apply the Science of Happiness to Accelerate Your Success*. New York: HarperCollins, 2016.

Stone, Douglas, Bruce Patton, and Sheila Heen. *Difficult Conversations*. New York: Viking, 1999.

"Women in the Workplace 2016 | McKinsey." Accessed September 5, 2019. https://www.mckinsey.com/business-functions/organization/our-insights/women-in-the-workplace-2016.

## About the Illustrator

Laura Sanders is an Ohio-built designer, illustrator, and comedian living in New Orleans.

As a sometimes too-confident child, Laura informed her parents she planned to "sell her drawings door-to-door." After a prolific high school career making T-shirts and posters for dances and musicals, she received a bachelor's degree in visual communication design from the Ohio State University.

Rather than knocking on doors with doodles after graduation, Laura has worked with liquor brands, big magazines, non-profits, bartender summer camps, software companies, comedy festivals, and many other weird and wonderful clients.

Laura is passionate about print layout and has received numerous awards from the Society of Professional Journalists for her work.

When she's not at her computer or on the couch with her dog Roscoe (he's a good boy), Laura performs stand-up across the country. Her album *Oh God Please Like Me* debuted at number one on the iTunes comedy charts. Laura regularly performs and produces comedy shows in New Orleans and would love to see you at one.

To find out about upcoming shows, say hello, or let Laura know about your favorite unlikely animal friendship, contact her at **www.laurasanders.fun**

## About the Author

Lelia (rhymes with "Amelia") started her company because women kept coming to her for support in professional negotiations and career decision-making.

Now a sought-after speaker, writer, and coach on workplace dynamics for women, Lelia remains an eternal optimist. She works with women who want to increase their impact and build more fulfilling and profitable careers.

Lelia writes regularly for publications including *Forbes*, *NBC News*, and *Harper's Bazaar*. As a former teen magazine enthusiast, she was particularly delighted when *Cosmopolitan* and *Marie Claire* profiled her for her strengths-based approach to negotiation.

Fortune 500 companies such as GE and Expedia, along with professional associations in fields from auto care to healthcare, hire her to support their teams.

With a Master's in Public Policy and a BA in Sociology, Lelia applies her understanding of political, professional, and cultural systems to support women in the workplace.

Finally, as a New Orleans native and enthusiast, Lelia freely uses the word *y'all*, has an entire closet dedicated to costuming, and brings the city's *joie de vivre* to all of her work.

Get in touch and find out more at
**www.leliagowland.com**

CPSIA information can be obtained
at www.ICGtesting.com
Printed in the USA
BVHW060316030522
635571BV00004B/9

9 781734 084702